ST. PAUL
ON THE POWER OF THE CROSS

Other Titles by Fr. Mitch Pacwa, S.J.:

The Proverbs Explained: A Blueprint for Christian Living

Wheat and Tares: Restoring the Moral Vision of a Scandalized Church

Available at:
WWW.EWTNRC.COM

Fr. Mitch Pacwa, S. J.

St. Paul on the Power of the Cross

EWTN Publishing, Inc.
Irondale, Alabama

The first edition of *St. Paul on the Power of the Cross* was published by Our Sunday Visitor, Inc. in 2008.

Cover by LUCAS Art & Design, Jenison, MI

Cover image: *Crucifixion with Madonna and Sts Paul, Mary Magdalene, John and Francis* by Bernardino Luini (WikiCommons)

Imprimi Potest
Very Reverend Edward W. Schmidt, S.J.
Provincial of the Chicago Province of the Society of Jesus
December 4, 2008

Nihil Obstat: Rev. Michael Heintz, Ph.D.
Censor Librorum

Imprimatur: ✠ John M. D'Arcy
Bishop of Fort Wayne–South Bend
November 10, 2008

The *Nihil Obstat* and *Imprimatur* are official declarations that a book or pamphlet is free of doctrinal or moral error. No implication is contained therein that those who have granted the *Nihil Obstat* or *Imprimatur* agree with the contents, opinions, or statements expressed.

EWTN Publishing, Inc.
5817 Old Leeds Road, Irondale, AL 35210

Distributed by Sophia Institute Press, Box 5284, Manchester, NH 03108.

paperback ISBN 978-1-68278-407-5

ebook ISBN 978-1-68278-408-2

Library of Congress Control Number: 2024944501

First printing

To Mother Angelica, P. C. P. A.,
who has evangelized like Paul
and has carried the Cross.

Contents

ST. PAUL
ON THE POWER OF THE CROSS

HOW TO USE THIS STUDY GUIDE IN A GROUP

This is an interactive study guide. It can be read with profit either alone or as part of a group Bible study. Below are suggestions for the use of this book in a group.

WHAT YOU WILL NEED FOR EVERY SESSION

- This study guide
- A Bible
- A notebook
- A pen or pencil

Before Session One, members of the group are encouraged to read the Introduction and Session One and to complete all the exercises in both. They should bring this study guide with them to the group session.

Begin the session with prayer (for example, A Prayer to the Apostle Paul).

Invite one person in the group to read one of the passages from St. Paul included in this session's material.

Allow five minutes of silent reflection on the passage. This allows the group to quiet their inner thoughts and to center themselves on the lesson to be discussed on St. Paul.

Catechesis: Give all members a chance to share some point that they have learned about St. Paul or the Cross, as discussed in the material. Was this something new or a new insight into something? Was there anything that raised a question? (Allow fifteen to twenty minutes for this.)

Discussion: Use the discussion questions at the end of the session's chapter to begin a deeper grasp of the material covered in the session. (Allow fifteen to twenty minutes for this.)

Conclusion: Have all members of the group summarize the key concepts they learned about St. Paul or the Cross, as discussed in the session. Assign the next session as homework, to be completed before the next group session.

THE SYMBOLS

 = Information

 = Stop and read

 = Writing exercise

 = Quotation

INTRODUCTION

THE CROSS OF JESUS

In his first letter to the Church at Corinth, St. Paul writes: "The word of the cross is folly to those who are perishing, but to us who are being saved it is the power of God" (1 Corinthians 1:18).

This little book is a study of an oft-repeated theme in Paul's letters: the centrality of the Cross of Jesus Christ for the salvation of souls. This theme reappears in a variety of contexts throughout the letters to explain the theology of salvation and the Church, his spirituality, and the dynamic of evangelization. In fact, most of the autobiographical material Paul wrote appears in those letters in which he speaks the most about his theology of the Cross. In these letters, he is usually confronting a pastoral problem caused by a variety of other evangelists bringing a changed form of the gospel into the churches he had established. Therefore we not only learn his theology of the Cross but also the way it affected his life.

We will examine these themes as a Bible study for you. Before we begin, however, you might want to take a little time to understand just what the Cross and crucifixion would have meant in the time of Paul.

CRUCIFIXION — A MOST WRETCHED DEATH

Crucifixion was a common form of execution for treason, sedition, or rebellion in the ancient world. One form of this horrible death began with the Assyrians, who impaled their victims, driving a spiked pole through the pelvis and into the chest. The Persians changed this by sometimes tying or nailing victims to crosses or stakes. The Romans developed it to a science.

> *i* A crucifixion victim was discovered in a Jewish burial site with the nail still embedded in the side of his ankle.

Crucifixion served two main purposes: 1) to create a shameful, painful death for the victim and 2) to be a deterrent to anyone who might be considering similar action. A runaway slave might be crucified, for instance, as a clear sign to all other slaves that such action would not be tolerated. Traitors and insurrectionists were frequently crucified. Spartacus is one of the most famous of these.

Crucifixion was frequently preceded by a scourging or beating intended to weaken the victim and hasten death since a healthy individual could live for several days hanging on a cross.

The condemned would carry his (rarely her) horizontal beam to the place of execution, where the upright would be permanently in place. Since crucifixion was the primary means of capital punishment in the Roman world, the process was streamlined as much as possible and having the vertical supports in place was more efficient than having to erect a new one each time. The victim was stripped naked, his hands and feet nailed or tied to the beams, and left to die.

> *i* Crucifixion was such a shameful death that Roman citizens were spared the humiliation of it. As a Roman citizen, Paul was executed by beheading.

The first century A.D. Jewish historian Josephus called crucifixion the "most wretched of deaths," and indeed, it was. Left exposed to the elements, to the derision of the crowds, and utterly helpless, the condemned suffered mercilessly. Death rarely came from loss of blood, but from muscle fatigue and exposure, which ultimately led to asphyxiation and heart failure. Victims usually died when they became too fatigued to push themselves up to take a breath; thus, in order to hasten death, the legs of the condemned would be broken — which is what happened to the thieves crucified with Jesus. In order to verify death, the centurion in charge of the execution would thrust a lance into the rib cage, administering the *coup de grace.* When this was done to Jesus, blood and water came from His side, indicating that He was truly dead.

In many parts of the ancient world, victims were often left hanging on the gibbet to be devoured by vultures and other wild beasts. Those who were removed were frequently discarded in common graves. In Palestine, however, Jewish law required the dead to be buried on the day of death, lest the land itself become polluted. For that reason, the corpses of the crucified were not left hanging but buried according to Jewish law. This was done for Jesus, especially since He died on the eve of a great feast, the Passover.

THE DEATH AND PASSION OF OUR LORD JESUS

Look up the passages listed below, and then describe what happened to Jesus as He was being tried and put to death on the Cross.

PASSAGE	EVENTS
Matthew 26:57	

PASSAGE	EVENTS
Mark 14:53–65	
Luke 23:8–9	
Matthew 27:26–31	
Matthew 27:34	
Luke 23:40–43	
Matthew 27:48	
Matthew 27:50	

THE APOSTLE PAUL

As a Pharisee trained in Judaism, Saul would find crucifixion abhorrent. The Old Testament teaches that anyone hung on a tree is accursed (Deuteronomy 21:23). As a Roman citizen exempt from the penalty of crucifixion, he would have been repelled by its horrible suffering and indignity. However, the power of the Cross in the lives of disciples became an essential component of the teaching of Paul. But before we can understand what he taught, we need to know a little about him.

Who was Paul? Born Saul in Tarsus in Asia Minor (modern Turkey), his parents were Israelites from the tribe of Benjamin. He was a Roman citizen, something that he would use to his advantage later in life (Acts 22:25–28). A tentmaker by profession (Acts 18:3), he was sent to Jerusalem to study under the highly esteemed Rabbi Gamaliel, a member of the Pharisee party of Jews (Acts 22:3). Gamaliel was so regarded as a scholar that when he died, it was said "the glory of the Law ceased and purity and abstinence died" (Mishna, Sotah 9:15).

Paul was, by his own account, a zealous young man who excelled in his studies (Galatians 1:14). His passion led him to actively persecute the early Christian Church, even participating in the murder of St. Stephen, the first martyr (Acts 7:58, 8:1). Having whetted his taste for ridding the world of Christians, he traveled to Damascus under the authorization of the chief priests in Jerusalem to arrest believers in that city. On the way there, however, he was struck blind by a vision of light that asked, "Saul, Saul, why do you persecute me?" The voice in the vision went on to say, "I am Jesus, whom you are persecuting" (Acts 9:4, 5). Following Jesus' instructions, Paul continued on to Damascus where he was baptized by Ananias (Acts 9:17).

> *i* Nowhere in Scripture does it say Paul was on a horse when he was traveling to Damascus.

Stop here and read Paul's account of his vision on the road to Damascus, in Acts 9:1–20.

The rest of his life was taken up with preaching the gospel. He was so fervent in his new passion that his life was frequently at risk (Acts 9:22–25). He returned to Jerusalem, then traveled to Tarsus, where the apostle Barnabas recruited him to help teach new Gentile (non-Jewish) converts in Antioch (Acts 11:25–26). From there, he and Barnabas traveled to Cyprus and Asia Minor and, on a second voyage, to Asia Minor and Europe. A third trip, and possibly a fourth, occurred after the accounts recorded in the Acts of the Apostles, which ends in A.D. 62 with Paul under house arrest in Rome, awaiting trial by the Emperor Nero. Paul was beheaded somewhere between A.D. 64 and 67. It has traditionally been believed that he was buried with St. Peter near the Via Appia until his remains were moved to what is now the Basilica of Saint Paul Outside-the-Walls in Rome.

THE JOURNEYS OF PAUL

Look up the passages listed in the table below, and then enter the names of some of the cities that Paul visited.

PASSAGE	EVENTS
Acts 13:4	

PASSAGE	EVENTS
Acts 13:46	
Acts 14:3	
Acts 14:19–24	
Acts 16:14–24	
Acts 18:5	
Acts 20:17–31	
Acts 28:11	

Session One

THE MESSAGE OF THE CROSS

1 Corinthians

CONSIDER

Paul's letters to the church at Corinth contain some of his most personal and intimate writings. 1 Corinthians, written while Paul was living in Ephesus, is the third of his letters. He wrote 1 and 2 Thessalonians while he was still dwelling in Corinth.

First Corinthians was prompted because Paul had received word of problems that had arisen since he left; he wanted both to correct abuses and to encourage and instruct the church he had founded.

In his letter, Paul gives us an inside look at some of the problems facing the nascent Christians, including factionalism, immorality, and liturgical abuses. The first issue that Paul addresses is the divisions that had developed within the young Christian community. These divisions were based on the Corinthians' ideas of the worth of certain apostles, evangelists, and teachers. Paul seeks to correct these views by highlighting the centrality of Jesus dying on the Cross. While the focus throughout these verses is on Paul's own preaching of the Cross, the Corinthians and by extension, all of us — are intended to take the next step and see the need to proclaim the Cross as not only the center of our lives but also the central message for the evangelization of other people.

STUDY

1 Corinthians 1:10–17

> [10]I appeal to you, brethren, by the name of our Lord
> Jesus Christ, that all of you agree and that there be no
> dissensions among you, but that you be united in the
> same mind and the same judgment. [11]For it has been
> reported to me by Chlo'e's people that there is quar-
> reling among you, my brethren. [12]What I mean is that
> each one of you says, "I belong to Paul," or "I belong to
> Apol'los," or "I belong to Cephas," or "I belong to Christ."
> [13]Is Christ divided? Was Paul crucified for you? Or were
> you baptized in the name of Paul? [14]I am thankful that I
> baptized none of you except Crispus and Ga'ius; [15]lest
> any one should say that you were baptized in my name.
> [16](I did baptize also the household of Steph'anas. Be-
> yond that, I do not know whether I baptized any one
> else.) [17]For Christ did not send me to baptize but to
> preach the gospel, and not with eloquent wisdom, lest
> the cross of Christ be emptied of its power.

Paul begins with a response to information brought to him by members of Chloe's household about certain divisions among the Corinthian Christians. We know almost nothing about Chloe, but perhaps her house was large enough for one of the Church community meetings. In that way she would be similar to Paul's first convert in Europe, Lydia of Philippi. The information Paul received talks about divisions that might well correspond to membership in various house churches. Since church buildings did not yet exist, it was typical for Christians to meet in each other's homes for instruction and celebration of the liturgy and other sacraments (see 1 Corinthians 11). However, meeting

THE GNOSTICS

The word "Gnostic" comes from the Greek meaning "knowledge." Around the second century, various sectarian movements developed erroneous teachings that, while they differed from one another, are collectively called Gnosticism. The main features include dualism—the idea that the spirit is good while matter is evil; the belief that the New Testament is for ordinary people, but true knowledge is received directly by elite spiritual people; this secret knowledge, not Jesus' death and Resurrection, is the means of enlightenment and thus salvation.

in different homes, with different preachers and teachers leading the groups, prompted some divisions within the community as a whole.

Chloe's representatives mentioned four divisions: the followers of Paul, who was now living in Ephesus; the followers of Apollos, who was still in Corinth; the followers of Cephas, which is the Aramaic word for Peter; and the followers of Christ. While it would seem logical that all Christians would follow Christ, this last named division may well have referred to a group that took the word "Christ" in its Greek sense of "an anointed person." As such these "Christ people" would claim to be endowed with a spirit of knowledge or wisdom that set them apart from the average Christian. If this interpretation is correct, these may have been an early form of Gnostics, who in the second century would write their own gospels based on claims to private spiritual knowledge that was superior to public revelation in Scripture. The Church would later excommunicate these Gnostics.

In his reply, Paul states that unity, not division, should characterize the Church. By this, he means that all members should speak the same thing about Christ, have the same mind and judgment, and make no divisions based on who preached the gospel to them. It is in this passage that Paul makes his first mention of the Cross of Christ (1:17) as he tries to explain that he was the first preacher, not the first baptizer, in the community. In fact, he mentions the very few people he did baptize to highlight the point that he did not try to baptize many others. That would be the task of Apollos. Paul will develop this point later in the letter, when he uses two images that show that he began the work and Apollos continued it.

> Stop here and look up 1 Corinthians 3:5–11. What images does Paul use to characterize his ministry and that of Apollos?

While Paul's mission was to "preach the gospel," he had a certain limit placed on him; he was not to use the "eloquent wisdom" of which the Greeks were so proud. He had tried using Greek philosophy as a tool for evangelization in Athens, but it did not succeed (see Acts 17:18–34). He had attempted to present the faith to the Stoic and Epicurean philosophers at the Areopagus. He even cited Greek philosophers, but the use of Greek wisdom only led to the philosophers mocking him or putting him off (17:32). By the time he came to

> Paul names the only two disciples that he himself baptized: Crispus and Gaius. Crispus was a synagogue ruler at Corinth who became a Christian. His conversion is mentioned in Acts 18:8. Gaius is referenced in Romans 16:23. He may be the same person as Titius Justus, with Gaius as a *praenomen*, or first name, at whose house Paul stayed when he was banned from the synagogue in Corinth.

Corinth, which was his next stop after Athens, he realized that such Greek wisdom did not work because it "emptied" the Cross of Christ of its power.

INVESTIGATE

The citizens of Athens took great pride in their philosophical learning and ability to debate. Read the following verses and note what happened when Paul tried to preach about Christ crucified to the Athenians.

PASSAGE	EVENT/REACTION
Acts 17:18	
Acts 17:19–21	
Acts 17:22–31	
Acts 17:32	
Acts 17:33	

PASSAGE	EVENT/REACTION
Acts 17:34	

Located in the same area as the Acropolis, which housed the Parthenon (the Temple of Athena), the Areopagus originally was a large stone hill where criminals could go to plead their cases with immunity. Later, it became a place where any person could express ideas without fear of arrest. Paul went there to explain the new teachings of Christianity.

STUDY

A. 1 Corinthians 1:18–25

18For the word of the cross is folly to those who are
perishing, but to us who are being saved it is the power
of God. 19For it is written, "I will destroy the wisdom of
the wise, and the cleverness of the clever I will thwart."
20Where is the wise man? Where is the scribe? Where
is the debater of this age? Has not God made foolish
the wisdom of the world? 21For since, in the wisdom
of God, the world did not know God through wisdom,
it pleased God through the folly of what we preach to
save those who believe. 22For Jews demand signs and
Greeks seek wisdom, 23but we preach Christ crucified,
a stumbling block to Jews and folly to Gentiles, 24but

> to those who are called, both Jews and Greeks, Christ the power of God and the wisdom of God. [25]For the foolishness of God is wiser than men, and the weakness of God is stronger than men.

In this section, Paul explains his rejection of human wisdom in favor of proclaiming that Jesus Christ crucified is the wisdom of God, and the Cross itself is the power of God. These verses lie at the heart of Paul's understanding of the importance of the Cross in our lives. Though everyone may be able to hear Paul's words, they have very different effects on different classes of hearers. People who are perishing — in other words, taking the way of sin — consider the Cross to be foolishness. However, those who are on the way to salvation understand the Cross as God's power.

Ironically, the fact that Christ crucified is a stumbling block to the Jews is itself a sign of Christ's authenticity, because it fulfills a prophecy in Isaiah 8:14–15.

Such a stark difference is not new. In the days of Moses, the wise enchanters of Egypt did not understand the power of God through Moses, the son of slaves and the leader of an enslaved people, until it was too late.

Stop here and read Exodus 7–10. As you read these passages, consider verse 19, which cites Isaiah 29:14: "Therefore, behold, I will again do marvelous things with this people, wonderful and marvelous; and the wisdom of their wise men shall perish, and the discernment of their discerning men shall be hid." Isaiah was criticizing Israel for pursuing an alliance with Egypt as a tactic for security from the Assyrian Empire. Isaiah belittles the Egyptians, who were famous for their sages and their magicians, yet were defeated by God in the days of Moses.

Consider the following: What is the role of the Egyptian magicians and sages throughout these episodes? At what point do the Egyptian wise men and magicians begin to lose face before the Lord? When do they admit their total defeat? What lesson might Paul be trying to teach by using this passage from Isaiah in regard to the wisdom of the Greeks in his own day?

B. 1 Corinthians 1:26–31

> 26For consider your call, brethren; not many of you
> were wise according to worldly standards, not many
> were powerful, not many were of noble birth; 27but
> God chose what is foolish in the world to shame the
> wise, God chose what is weak in the world to shame
> the strong, 28God chose what is low and despised in
> the world, even things that are not, to bring to noth-
> ing things that are, 29so that no human being might
> boast in the presence of God. 30 He is the source of
> your life in Christ Jesus, whom God made our wisdom,
> our righteousness and sanctification and redemption,
> 31therefore, as it is written, "Let him who boasts, boast
> in the Lord."

Paul makes several points in this passage, all of which ultimately relate to the power of the Cross. His first point is that God's plan to use that which seems weak and foolish to the world does not apply solely to the redemption of humanity through the death of Jesus. Remember that crucifixion represented the most shameful sort of death. Only the most wretched of criminals were subjected to it. To the citizens of the ancient world, anyone who was crucified was to be disregarded and despised. Paul stresses that just as the death of Jesus turned the idea of weakness into strength, so, too, God's choosing of the weak and foolish to become the recipients of the gospel of the Cross is intended to embarrass the powerful and wise.

In 1:30–31, Paul strengthens his idea that the weakness and foolishness of the Corinthian Christians is an important aspect of God's plan, just as the Crucifixion of Jesus was an essential part of God's plan. Paul points out that the Corinthian Christians — indeed, all Christians — are in Christ, an idea he learned when he met Christ on the road to Damascus. At that time, Jesus asked him why he was persecuting "Me," when all that Paul (called Saul at the time) saw was that he was trying to eliminate a heretical Jewish sect. He did not understand that by persecuting the Christians, he was persecuting Christ himself. Through his experience, which is recounted in Acts 9, Saul learned how profoundly Christ identifies himself with the members of his Church. For that reason he writes that the Corinthian Christians (and, indeed, all of us) are in Christ. He will develop this idea much more extensively in 1 Corinthians 12, when he speaks of the Church as the Body of Christ.

The second point Paul makes in this passage is that Jesus, through His life and ultimate death on the Cross, personifies God's wisdom and holiness. Later in 1 Corinthians 6:11, holiness (or its related word, being "sanctified") is connected with being "justified" in Baptism.

i In the Old Testament, "sanctification" or "holiness" is connected especially with God and the celebration of the liturgies in the temple (see Exodus 29:42–44, where the tent constructed for worship and offering sacrifice will be the place to meet the Lord and be "sanctified," or made holy, by his "glory"). Paul identifies Jesus as the personal source of all holiness, as opposed to the Tent of Meeting or the Temple, which was limited to one site (Jerusalem since the time of David) and to one people, namely, Israel. Since Christ personifies holiness, any person, Jew or Gentile, male or female, slave or free, can have faith in Jesus Christ crucified, be joined to Him in Baptism, and thus be in the presence of His holiness.

A third point Paul makes is that Jesus personifies "righteousness." This is the same word translated as "justification" in some other texts. Normally, the Old Testament meaning refers to the norm of life by which humans conform to God's expectations. Sometimes, it even means "victory" in battle or vindication in the courtroom. However, since Jesus is its personification, righteousness is not something but, rather, Someone.

Part of Paul's message is that Christ became these qualities for the sake of sinful humanity so that they might become what Christ became for them. Since Christ personifies wisdom, holiness, and righteousness, He is able to bring these qualities into those who are united with Him through the sacrifice of the Cross.

Fourth, since Christ personifies true wisdom, holiness, and righteousness, those Christians who belong to Him and are in Him have no reason to boast. Paul commands the Corinthians to remain humble, following the prophet Jeremiah's advice (9:24), precisely because they had been boasting in human beings — Paul, Apollos, and Cephas. By implication, they were boasting about their own abilities to choose the better leaders. Here, Paul orders them to boast only in the Lord Jesus Christ, who personifies the wisdom, holiness, and righteousness of God, the true power of the Cross.

INVESTIGATE

The personification of wisdom began in the Old Testament, where it is portrayed as a woman, since the Hebrew word for *wisdom*, as with the great majority of abstract nouns, is a feminine word. (Hebrew has only two genders: masculine and feminine). Look up some of the texts that personify wisdom:

PASSAGE	CHARACTERISTICS
Proverbs 1:20ff	
Proverbs 8	
Proverbs 9:1–3	
Wisdom 6:7ff	
Wisdom 9:1ff, especially v. 3	

PASSAGE	CHARACTERISTICS
Wisdom 10	
Sirach 1	
Sirach 24	

STUDY

A. 1 Corinthians 2:1–5

> 1When I came to you, brethren, I did not come pro-
> claiming to you the testimony of God in lofty words
> or wisdom. 2For I decided to know nothing among
> you except Jesus Christ and him crucified. 3And I was
> with you in weakness and in much fear and trembling;
> 4and my speech and my message were not in plausible
> words of wisdom, but in demonstration of the Spirit and
> power, 5that your faith might not rest in the wisdom of
> men but in the power of God.

Paul recalls that his personal experience among the Corinthians, at the start of his ministry, actually exemplified the teaching he just presented to them in the previous verses. He did not use lofty wisdom when bringing his message. Instead, he spoke of nothing except Jesus Christ crucified. Paul felt himself to be weak and in fear and trembling, not unlike Christ from His agony in Gethsemane until His final cry on the Cross. Paul emphasizes that he shares Christ's weakness, and this weakness and death on the Cross is his message. Yet, in Paul's weakness, the power and manifestation of the Holy Spirit was present, making it clear that God is the one who brings conversion. God is the source of the power in Paul's weakness, and God is the object of faith for the Corinthians. Since this was the basis of Paul's success among them, then they should continue the same proclamation of Christ rather than boast in human teachers.

> Jesus Christ taught that when He was lifted up, He would draw all men to Himself—a reference to the manner in which He would die on the Cross (John 12:31–33). Just as Jesus emphasized that His death would draw all people to Himself, so does Paul.

B. 1 Corinthians 2:6–16

> [6]Yet among the mature we do impart wisdom, although
> it is not a wisdom of this age or of the rulers of this age,
> who are doomed to pass away. [7]But we impart a secret
> and hidden wisdom of God, which God decreed before
> the ages for our glorification. [8]None of the rulers of this
> age understood this; for if they had, they would not
> have crucified the Lord of glory. [9]But, as it is written,
> "What no eye has seen, nor ear heard, nor the heart of
> man conceived, what God has prepared for those who
> love him," [10]God has revealed to us through the Spirit.

> For the Spirit searches everything, even the depths of
> God. 11For what person knows a man's thoughts except
> the spirit of the man which is in him? So also no one
> comprehends the thoughts of God except the Spirit
> of God. 12Now we have received not the spirit of the
> world, but the Spirit which is from God, that we might
> understand the gifts bestowed on us by God. 13And we
> impart this in words not taught by human wisdom but
> taught by the Spirit, interpreting spiritual truths to those
> who possess the Spirit.
>
> 14The unspiritual man does not receive the gifts of the
> Spirit of God, for they are folly to him, and he is not
> able to understand them because they are spiritually
> discerned. 15The spiritual man judges all things, but is
> himself to be judged by no one. 16"For who has known
> the mind of the Lord so as to instruct him?" But we
> have the mind of Christ.

Here, Paul recognizes that our desire for wisdom is not inappropriate, so long as we seek the wisdom of God. However, God's wisdom does not belong to the present world or culture because it is a "mystery," or hidden wisdom. (The word translated as "secret" is the Greek term *mysterion,* from which we get our word *mystery.*) On one hand, people cannot understand God's eternal wisdom because their sin blinds them to seeing God's plans. Their blindness is so thorough that they even crucified the Lord of glory who had been sent to redeem them from their folly.

i The source of the quote in verse 9 is unknown, but it is similar to Isaiah 64:4: "From of old no one has heard or perceived by the ear, no eye has seen a God besides thee, who works for those who wait for him." The Fathers of the Church, particularly Jerome, Ambrosiaster, and Origen, suggest that it is a quote from the *Secrets of Elijah*. However, it is not known in the existing fragment of that work.

Another aspect of this wisdom is that God intends it to give glory to human beings. The glory is not simply some form of honor. Rather, glory in the Old Testament refers to the power of God's presence, especially in the Temple, also present in the Lord that the rulers had crucified.

C. 1 Corinthians 5:1–11

> [1]It is actually reported that there is immorality among
> you, and of a kind that is not found even among pagans;
> for a man is living with his father's wife. [2]And you are
> arrogant! Ought you not rather to mourn? Let him who
> has done this be removed from among you. [3]For though
> absent in body I am present in spirit, and as if present,
> I have already pronounced judgment [4]in the name of
> the Lord Jesus on the man who has done such a thing.
> When you are assembled, and my spirit is present, with
> the power of our Lord Jesus, [5]you are to deliver this man
> to Satan for the destruction of the flesh, that his spirit
> may be saved in the day of the Lord Jesus. [6]Your boasting
> is not good. Do you not know that a little leaven leavens
> the whole lump? [7]Cleanse out the old leaven that you
> may be a new lump, as you really are unleavened. For
> Christ, our paschal lamb, has been sacrificed. [8]Let us,
> therefore, celebrate the festival, not with the old leaven,

> the leaven of malice and evil, but with the unleavened
> bread of sincerity and truth. [9]I wrote to you in my letter
> not to associate with immoral men; [10]not at all meaning
> the immoral of this world, or the greedy and robbers,
> or idolaters, since then you would need to go out of the
> world. [11]But rather I wrote to you not to associate with
> any one who bears the name of brother if he is guilty of
> immorality or greed, or is an idolater, reviler, drunkard,
> or robber — not even to eat with such a one.

While this passage does not seem to deal with the Cross on first reading, its deeper meaning can be understood as we examine the Sacrificial Mystery of the Eucharist. Paul relates Jesus' death on the Cross to the Old Testament sacrifices, particularly those of Passover.

The first step in understanding this passage is to understand the scandalous situation that Paul is addressing. A man was cohabiting with his father's wife. Presumably this was not the man's mother, but a subsequent wife of his father. Other details are not known: Had his father died? Did the woman depend on the stepson for material support? Nonetheless, no excuse could be accepted since this kind of incestuous relationship had been prohibited by earlier laws:

> Stop here and look up the following passages, which Paul would certainly have known from his Rabbinic training: Leviticus 18:18; Leviticus 20:11; Deuteronomy 22:30; Deuteronomy 27:20.

Paul warns of the negative influence this incestuous Christian might have on the whole community, illustrating this with the image of a little bit of leaven influencing the whole lump of dough. Likewise, tolerating even this one public scandal of serious sin could spread throughout the whole community and influence other members to commit sin by being permissive.

Paul then jumps to a second image regarding leaven, this time at the Passover. To this day, Jewish people carefully scour their homes and businesses to remove any and all forms of leaven from the place before the Feast of Passover begins. They even sell beer at an incredible discount so as to remove the yeast with which it is fermented from the premises. This pre-Passover cleansing is Paul's image for the removal of the public scandal from the midst of the community.

Then, because he is discussing the removal of all leaven at Passover, he highlights the importance of the removal of the scandal by linking it with the presence of Christ, our Passover Lamb. Just as the presence of the Passover lamb and the leaven were incompatible with the celebration of the great Jewish feast, so also is the presence of the leaven of sin incompatible with the presence of Jesus Christ in the Church.

An important element of this text is that Paul recognizes the death of Jesus on the Cross as a sacrifice, parallel to the sacrifice of the Passover lambs. This acknowledges that the death of Jesus is no merely heroic act, nor is it some tragedy inflicted on a great man. Rather, His death on the Cross is a sacrifice that Christians continue to celebrate. Of course, this will be primarily celebrated in the Eucharist.

> *i* "Paschal" is an adjective used to describe anything associated with the Passover. This word comes from the Hebrew word Pesach, which means "Passover." That Hebrew word passed over as a loan word into Greek and from there into Latin and English. Therefore, we speak of Paschaltide, the Paschal lamb, and many other terms associated with Christ's "passover" from death to Resurrection.

Jesus as the Paschal sacrifice is directly linked to the time of Jesus' Crucifixion, which occurred between noon and 3:00 p.m. The Passover lambs were being slain in the Temple while Jesus was hanging on the Cross. The blood of those lambs was sprinkled on doorposts and lintels while Jesus' blood flowed on his Cross. The blood of the lambs was meant to protect Israel from the angel of death; the blood of Jesus Christ, shed on the Cross, saves us from sin and eternal death in Hell.

> Stop here and read 1 Corinthians 11:1–22. As with so many other issues in this letter, Paul is responding to a question that had been presented to him by the envoys from Corinth. What were the abuses taking place in the liturgy? What does Paul suggest to correct these abuses?

D. 1 Corinthians 11:23–32

> 23For I received from the Lord what I also delivered
> to you, that the Lord Jesus on the night when he was
> betrayed took bread, 24and when he had given thanks,
> he broke it, and said, "This is my body which is for you.
> Do this in remembrance of me." 25In the same way also
> the cup, after supper, saying, "This cup is the new covenant in my blood. Do this, as often as you drink it,
> in remembrance of me." 26For as often as you eat this
> bread and drink the cup, you proclaim the Lord's death
> until he comes.
>
> 27Whoever, therefore, eats the bread or drinks the cup
> of the Lord in an unworthy manner will be guilty of

> profaning the body and blood of the Lord. [28] Let a man examine himself, and so eat of the bread and drink of the cup. [29]For any one who eats and drinks without discerning the body eats and drinks judgment upon himself. [30]That is why many of you are weak and ill, and some have died. [31]But if we judged ourselves truly, we should not be judged. [32]But when we are judged by the Lord, we are chastened so that we may not be condemned along with the world.

Paul continues his teaching on the Eucharist by declaring that his understanding came from the tradition he had received from the Christians before him. He passed on this tradition to the Corinthians about how to celebrate the Eucharist, based on what Jesus did on the night before He died. Even the separation of the actions of consecrating the Body and then the Blood of Christ is a symbolic indication of death — when someone's body is separate from the blood, the person is dead. However, Paul makes this explicit in 11:26 by declaring that receiving the Body and Blood of Christ is a proclamation of His death until the end of the world, when Jesus comes again.

Finally, Paul returns to his theme of the abuses at the liturgy. Unworthy reception of the Eucharist is a profanation of the Body and Blood of Christ and a diminution of the sacrifice of the Cross. Consequently, to receive the Eucharist unworthily incurs a judgment against the person who does so.

E. 1 Corinthians 15:1–11

> [1]Now I would remind you, brethren, in what terms I preached to you the gospel, which you received, in which you stand, [2]by which you are saved, if you hold it fast — unless you believed in vain. [3]For I delivered

> to you as of first importance what I also received, that
> Christ died for our sins in accordance with the scrip-
> tures, 4that he was buried, that he was raised on the
> third day in accordance with the scriptures, 5and that
> he appeared to Cephas, then to the twelve. 6Then he
> appeared to more than five hundred brethren at one
> time, most of whom are still alive, though some have
> fallen asleep. 7Then he appeared to James, then to all
> the apostles. 8Last of all, as to one untimely born, he
> appeared also to me. 9For I am the least of the apostles,
> unfit to be called an apostle, because I persecuted the
> church of God. 10But by the grace of God I am what I
> am, and his grace toward me was not in vain. On the
> contrary, I worked harder than any of them, though
> it was not I, but the grace of God which is with me.
> 11Whether then it was I or they, so we preach and so
> you believed.

The main thrust of 15:1–11 is to enumerate the various appearances of Christ after the Resurrection. The point is to mention the witnesses, most of whom were still alive at the time of writing this letter — just a little more than twenty years after the actual event of Resurrection. Note, however, that in this passage about the Resurrection, the first event is that Christ died on the Cross for our sins and was buried in accordance with the Scripture. The importance of the death of Christ and the power of the Cross is highlighted immediately.

INVESTIGATE

Read all of 1 Corinthians 15. Note the false ideas held by some of the Corinthians about Christ's Resurrection from the dead and list them here:

PASSAGE	BELIEFS
1 Corinthians 15:12–19	
1 Corinthians 15:30–34	
1 Corinthians 15:35–44	
1 Corinthians 15:50–58	

DISCUSS

1. How do the scandals and abuses among the Corinthians relate to modern scandals and abuses? How does Paul's advice apply to us today?

2. Paul writes: "We preach Christ crucified, a stumbling block to Jews and folly to Gentiles." Have you ever found the Cross to be a stumbling block? Have you ever considered it folly or foolishness? Are you ever embarrassed to admit you are a Christian when you are in the company of the worldly wise?

3. What do you say when someone challenges your Catholic Faith? How do you respond when a non-Christian confronts you about your beliefs?

PRACTICE

What is the message of the Cross in your own life? How can you make your life a living witness to the power of the Cross?

Session Two

SUFFERING AND THE CROSS

2 Corinthians

CONSIDER

Paul frequently refers to his sufferings for the sake of the gospel, seeing his experiences as a living out the message of the Cross. Many modern Christians look to him as the source for their theology of salvation. They believe that being justified by faith in the death of Jesus Christ on the Cross leads to the comforting assertion that Jesus did all the suffering for me; I simply need to accept this free gift from God by faith alone. However, Paul disagrees, seeing his own suffering as an integral part of Christian growth. In fact, Paul's claim to be a servant of Christ is based, not on his own list of miracles and wonders — which, according to the Acts of the Apostles, would be reasonably easy for him to do — but on his suffering and persecution for Christ as his credentials. For Paul, the power of the Cross is the central source not only of faith, but power for living. In uniting with the Cross, we die to self, only to live with Christ.

The theology of salvation is known as *soteriology.* Soteriology examines how the merits of the Incarnation, death, and Resurrection of Christ effect our salvation, as well as how we become righteous, holy, and sanctified. The thorniest issues concern the role of God's grace and its relationship to human free will.

> Stop here and preview the account of Paul's sufferings in 2 Corinthians 11:23–29.

STUDY

A. 2 Corinthians 1:1–2

> 1 Paul, an apostle of Christ Jesus by the will of God, and
> Timothy our brother: To the church of God which is
> at Corinth, with all the saints who are in the whole of
> Acha'ia: 2 Grace to you and peace from God our Father
> and the Lord Jesus Christ.

Paul opens his second letter to the Corinthians with a traditional greeting, which identifies the senders as Paul and Timothy and the recipients as the Church of God at Corinth. He identifies himself as "an apostle of Christ Jesus by the will of God." This title is connected to a chief concern of the letter — namely, that Paul's role and authority as an apostle had been brought into question by some unnamed opponents who claim to be "super apostles" (11:5). This is quite different from his motivation for the first letter to the Corinthians, where he confronted issues of moral behavior and incorrect doctrine.

In this letter, he defends himself against attacks on his authority as an apostle. More importantly, we can observe the development of his thought on the meaning of being a true apostle and apply it to our own lives and self-understanding. As we examine passages in this letter, we see how Paul defends his authority by developing a theology of the death and Resurrection of Christ. Through his personal struggles, we come to a clearer understanding of the real meaning and power of the Cross.

B. 2 Corinthians 1:3–14

[3]Blessed be the God and Father of our Lord Jesus Christ,
the Father of mercies and God of all comfort, [4]who
comforts us in all our affliction, so that we may be able
to comfort those who are in any affliction, with the
comfort with which we ourselves are comforted by God.
[5]For as we share abundantly in Christ's sufferings, so
through Christ we share abundantly in comfort too. [6]If
we are afflicted, it is for your comfort and salvation; and
if we are comforted, it is for your comfort, which you
experience when you patiently endure the same suffer-
ings that we suffer. [7]Our hope for you is unshaken; for
we know that as you share in our sufferings, you will
also share in our comfort.

[8]For we do not want you to be ignorant, brethren, of the
affliction we experienced in Asia; for we were so utterly,
unbearably crushed that we despaired of life itself. [9]Why,
we felt that we had received the sentence of death; but
that was to make us rely not on ourselves but on God
who raises the dead; [10]he delivered us from so deadly
a peril, and he will deliver us; on him we have set our
hope that he will deliver us again. [11]You also must help
us by prayer, so that many will give thanks on our behalf
for the blessing granted us in answer to many prayers.

[12]For our boast is this, the testimony of our conscience
that we have behaved in the world, and still more toward
you, with holiness and godly sincerity, not by earthly
wisdom but by the grace of God. [13]For we write you
nothing but what you can read and understand; I hope

> you will understand fully, [14]as you have understood in part, that you can be proud of us as we can be of you, on the day of the Lord Jesus.

This section of the letter is a thanksgiving, which is also a traditional component of ancient letters (including most of Paul's). He proclaims God the Father blessed; however, the titles he gives God — the Father of our Lord Jesus Christ, the Father of mercies, and God of comfort — are followed by the assertion that God is our comfort. Paul explains that God's comfort is a gift that enables him not only to endure his suffering but to comfort others.

> (i) Apparently, one of the criticisms made by Paul's opponents is that if he were a true apostle, God would protect him from suffering. In their eyes, his suffering and persecution were an indication of the lack of God's favor.

C. 2 Corinthians 4:5–13

> [5]For what we preach is not ourselves, but Jesus Christ
> as Lord, with ourselves as your servants for Jesus' sake.
> [6]For it is the God who said, "Let light shine out of dark-
> ness," who has shone in our hearts to give the light of
> the knowledge of the glory of God in the face of Christ.
>
> [7]But we have this treasure in earthen vessels, to show
> that the transcendent power belongs to God and not
> to us. [8]We are afflicted in every way, but not crushed;
> perplexed, but not driven to despair; [9]persecuted, but
> not forsaken; struck down, but not destroyed; [10]always
> carrying in the body the death of Jesus, so that the life of

> Jesus may also be manifested in our bodies. [11]For while
> we live we are always being given up to death for Jesus'
> sake, so that the life of Jesus may be manifested in our
> mortal flesh. [12]So death is at work in us, but life in you.
>
> [13]Since we have the same spirit of faith as he had who
> wrote, "I believed, and so I spoke," we too believe, and
> so we speak.

While the "super apostles" make themselves and their successes an object of their message, Paul insists that Jesus Christ crucified and resurrected is the point of his preaching. He emphasizes that he is simply someone in whose heart "the light of the knowledge of the glory of God has shone in the face of Christ." At the same time, the light is held in a clay vessel, which highlights Paul's fragility and weakness in the presence of God's surpassing and abundant power.

To further highlight his weakness, Paul gives the first of three lists of his suffering and affliction. He presents his weaknesses in pairs of words, the second part of which indicates that his weakness is real but it is never so overwhelming as to completely destroy him. He then explains that these weaknesses are precisely the way he is always bearing the death of Jesus in his own body. In other words, contrary to the claims of the "super apostles" that Paul is an inadequate apostle due to his weaknesses, Paul presents his difficulties as the means of his union with the death and Resurrection of Jesus. It is precisely through our weakness and suffering, Paul says, that the power of the Cross will be made manifest in our own bodies.

INVESTIGATE

To help understand Paul's point about the light being carried in a clay vessel, read Judges 7:16–21. The hero of this passage is Gideon, who is the youngest member of his family, belonging to the youngest clan in his tribe, which is the youngest tribe in Israel. All that information adds up to him being the lowest man among the tribes of Israel. Answer the following:

What is Gideon's tribe and clan?

Against which oppressors did Gideon lead the Israelites in battle?

What was the role of light in clay vessels in winning the victory?

Paul also proclaims a link between the abundant share in Christ's sufferings and the share in His comfort. The more we share in Christ's suffering, the more we share in His comfort. Yet the reception of comfort has another side. We must also share that comfort with other suffering and afflicted Christians. In that way, not only will the comfort we — like Paul — receive from God comfort them, but it will also be for their salvation as they patiently endure their sufferings.

Finally, Paul explains that the reason death works in his body is so that life may be given to the Corinthians. His belief that his suffering can benefit the Corinthians is strongly connected to his idea that the Church is the mystical body of Christ (1 Corinthians 12). If everyone is a member of Christ, and if every member is connected to one another by the Holy Spirit, then the suffering of one member may benefit the other members. For instance, if one part of a body — say, a finger — is cut, then it feels pain and fights infection so that the rest of the body does not suffer from gangrene or blood poisoning. In the same way, the suffering of one member of the Church may benefit other members.

> "Thus to share in the sufferings of Christ is, at the same time, to suffer for the Kingdom of God. In the eyes of the just God, before his judgment, those who share in the suffering of Christ become worthy of this Kingdom."
>
> — Pope John Paul II, *Salvifici Doloris (On the Christian Meaning of Human Suffering)*, 1984.

D. 2 Corinthians 5:1–11

> [1]For we know that if the earthly tent we live in is destroyed, we have a building from God, a house not made with hands, eternal in the heavens. [2]Here indeed we groan, and long to put on our heavenly dwelling, [3]so that by putting it on we may not be found naked. [4]For while we are still in this tent, we sigh with anxiety; not that we would be unclothed, but that we would be further clothed, so that what is mortal may be swallowed up by life. [5]He who has prepared us for this very thing is God, who has given us the Spirit as a guarantee.
>
> [6]So we are always of good courage; we know that while we are at home in the body we are away from the Lord, [7]for we walk by faith, not by sight. [8]We are of good courage, and we would rather be away from the body and at home with the Lord. [9]So whether we are at home or away, we make it our aim to please him. [10]For we must all appear before the judgment seat of Christ, so that each one may receive good or evil, according to what he has done in the body.
>
> [11]Therefore, knowing the fear of the Lord, we persuade men; but what we are is known to God, and I hope it is known also to your conscience.

Once he has established the link between our suffering and Christ's suffering on the Cross, Paul begins to further develop his theology of the Cross. Whereas he spoke of the human body as the temple of the Holy Spirit in 1 Corinthians 6:19, now he speaks of the body as an earthly tent.

Paul says that life in this world is inevitably painful, as we long for eternal life in Heaven, where the pain will be no more. He longs for eternal life but does not want to be found naked. What might this mean? Apparently Paul longs for the resurrection of the body at the end of time, when the eternal temple of heaven will be our dwelling place. However, if a Christian dies before the general resurrection, the soul will dwell with God, though without the earthly mortal body or the glorified body. Paul portrays the existence of the bodyless soul in heaven as a nakedness.

In the midst of this "anxiety," Paul offers a profound encouragement: God offers the Holy Spirit as a type of down payment or guarantee that He will accomplish the redemption of our bodies. Even though the total reality of the future life of redemption is not yet clear, we walk by faith, which is itself a gift from God, believing that our earthly lives will not end in death any more than Christ's life ended in death. In joining with Christ's death on the Cross, we ultimately will join with Him in His Resurrection — both body and soul.

While such thought offers amazing encouragement, Paul also reminds us of the coming judgment of all the deeds we have done in this life. This means that life in this mortal tent is extremely significant, even if it is short in comparison to eternal life in Heaven. We perform good and evil deeds. Christ will judge these deeds with truth, thorough justice, and infinite mercy. The proper attitude to take is "fear of the Lord." No one can take the mercy for granted; neither can a person earn his way to salvation. Paul insists that we have this fear of the Lord in mind as we persuade others to follow the life in Christ. If we do not have this fear of the Lord, we may preach to them yet avoid living the truth of holy and good lives ourselves.

INVESTIGATE

We are familiar with John 1:14, which usually is translated as "The word became flesh and dwelt among us." But the Greek word translated as "dwelt" is, literally, "he tented." Look up the following verses and see what they have to say about tents and temples.

PASSAGE	DESCRIPTION
Exodus 25:40	
Exodus 26:30	
Exodus 27:8	
Numbers 8:4	
Acts 7:44	
Hebrews 8:1–5	

STUDY

2 Corinthians 5:12–17

> [12]We are not commending ourselves to you again but
> giving you cause to be proud of us, so that you may be
> able to answer those who pride themselves on a man's
> position and not on his heart. [13]For if we are beside
> ourselves, it is for God; if we are in our right mind, it
> is for you. [14]For the love of Christ controls us, because
> we are convinced that one has died for all; therefore
> all have died. [15]And he died for all, that those who live
> might live no longer for themselves but for him who
> for their sake died and was raised.
>
> [16]From now on, therefore, we regard no one from a
> human point of view; even though we once regarded
> Christ from a human point of view, we regard him thus
> no longer. [17]Therefore, if any one is in Christ, he is a
> new creation; the old has passed away, behold, the new
> has come.

Having looked at suffering, death, and the resurrection of the body as part of his theology of the Cross, Paul returns to the sore subject of the "super apostles" who are trying to discredit his ministry. He commends himself, not to boast but to defend himself as a preacher of the authentic gospel of Christ. That is why he wants the Corinthians to be proud of him. Apparently, the "super apostles" have caused them some shame for having been committed to Paul, but Paul wants the Corinthians to be proud of him and his authentic teachings. Paul insists that his heart is right. This is especially important in light of what he wrote about standing before the judgment seat of Christ.

The love of Christ controls his heart and his whole life, and that is what the Corinthians should be proud of in knowing Paul.

At the same time, he does not neglect his theology of the Cross. He is "convinced that one has died for all" and so "all have died" (5:14) as the basis for the love of Christ controlling his heart. This verse lies at the heart of his willingness to boast of his suffering. While the "super apostles" consider success and prosperity to be indicators of their status as "super," Paul sees that Christ's death for all requires all to die with Him. Therefore, his sufferings and tribulations are not signs of failure but of authentic union with Jesus Christ.

Furthermore, in 5:15, Paul says that all Christians are to live for Jesus Christ, who "died for their sake and was raised." Christ and His Cross must be the focal point of all activity by Christians. Finally, Paul refutes another argument of the "super apostles." Apparently, they claimed to have known Jesus during His earthly ministry. They may have claimed to have seen His miracles and perhaps even witnessed His death and Resurrection. However, Paul's commitment to dying with Jesus and living His sufferings is more important than having seen Jesus during His earthly ministry. In fact, based on the Gospel record of the negative reactions of the crowds to Jesus, knowledge of Him during the earthly ministry may not be such a good qualification after all.

INVESTIGATE

What else does Paul say about suffering and the role it plays in our lives as Christians? Look at these passages and note some of the key ideas he presents for dealing with suffering in our daily lives.

PASSAGE	KEY CONCEPTS
Romans 5:3	
Romans 8:17	
Romans 12:1–2	
Colossians 1:24	
Philippians 3:10	
2 Thessalonians 1:5	

STUDY

2 Corinthians 5:18–21

> 18 All this is from God, who through Christ reconciled
> us to himself and gave us the ministry of reconcilia-
> tion; 19 that is, God was in Christ reconciling the world
> to himself, not counting their trespasses against them,
> and entrusting to us the message of reconciliation. 20 So
> we are ambassadors for Christ, God making his appeal
> through us. We beseech you on behalf of Christ, be
> reconciled to God. 21 For our sake he made him to be
> sin who knew no sin, so that in him we might become
> the righteousness of God.

In these verses, Paul defines his apostolic role. He is not the center of attention, as was the case for the "super apostles." Rather, he is simply an ambassador of God, that is, someone who announces the message given to him by his sovereign, who is God. The message he brings is the reconciliation of the world to God through the death and Resurrection of Jesus Christ. Therefore, Paul summons the Corinthians to be reconciled to God through the power of the Cross.

The message of the Cross appears when Paul explains the basis on which Jesus reconciles the world. God made Christ to be "sin," even though Jesus knew no sin. By this process we become "the righteousness of God," which is the meaning of the reconciliation with God. What does this verse mean?

First, Paul maintains the New Testament view that Jesus did not know sin. In the Old Testament one knows something by experiencing it. Thus Paul is saying that Jesus did not experience sin or have personal knowledge of sin by committing any.

INVESTIGATE

Look up the following passages that indicate Jesus is sinless. Show how these verses are connected with the prophecy in Isaiah 53:9.

PASSAGE	CONNECTION WITH ISAIAH
Hebrews 4:15	
Hebrews 7:26	
1 Peter 2:22–24	
1 John 3:5	

Second, the statement that "God made him to be sin" is also based on Old Testament language. Leviticus describes a variety of types of sacrifice: peace offering, thanksgiving offering, guilt offering, and sin offering. Sometimes the word "offering" is not actually stated in the Hebrew text, so the word is simply "sin" or "guilt." In this context, Paul is saying that Jesus became an offering for sin.

INVESTIGATE

A number of passages in the Old Testament describe the sin offerings, particularly at the feast of the Day of Atonement. Look up the follow passages:

- Exodus 30:10
- Leviticus 16:5–6

What are the factors that affect the differences in the kind of animal sacrificed?

What are the occasions of sin that require a sin offering?

Third, the effect of Jesus becoming a sin offering for the sake of us sinners is that He can transform us into the righteousness of God. In other words, He can change the state of our souls into a righteousness that is similar to His. This is no mere external imputation. Rather, Christ effects a true transformation of the person who believes in him — an interior transformation to make us into new creations modeled on the original righteousness of the first human beings at the time of the first creation. Through His death, we can become new again.

STUDY

2 Corinthians 6:1–10

> [1]Working together with him, then, we entreat you not
> to accept the grace of God in vain. [2]For he says, "At the
> acceptable time I have listened to you, and helped you
> on the day of salvation." Behold, now is the acceptable
> time; behold, now is the day of salvation. [3]We put no
> obstacle in any one's way, so that no fault may be found
> with our ministry, [4]but as servants of God we commend
> ourselves in every way: [4b]through great endurance, in
> afflictions, hardships, calamities, [5]beatings, imprison-
> ments, tumults, [5b]labors, watching, hunger; [6]by purity,
> knowledge, forbearance, kindness, the Holy Spirit,
> genuine love, [7]truthful speech, and the power of God;
> with the weapons of righteousness for the right hand
> and for the left; [8]in honor and dishonor, in ill repute and
> good repute. We are treated as impostors, and yet are
> true; [9]as unknown, and yet well known; as dying, and
> behold we live; as punished, and yet not killed; [10]as sor-
> rowful, yet always rejoicing; as poor, yet making many
> rich; as having nothing, and yet possessing everything.

This text summarizes Paul's experiences of a wide variety of suffering, virtues, and a set of paradoxes regarding his reputation and actual life. Oddly, he understands these experiences, including the pain, as God's "acceptable time" and the "day of salvation." He cites these terms from Isaiah 49:8, the second of Isaiah's four "Songs of the Servant of the Lord," which are applied to Christ throughout the New Testament. In 5:21, Paul had linked Jesus' death on the Cross as a sin offering to the Fourth Song of the Servant of the Lord (Isaiah 52:13–53:12). In the followup passage, Paul links the second Servant Song to himself because he shares in Christ's role as a suffering servant. Not only does he defend himself against the "super apostles" here, but he also invites the Corinthians — and, indeed, all Christians — to share in the same suffering servant role of Christ crucified.

STUDY

A. 2 Corinthians 11:1–4

> [1]I wish you would bear with me in a little foolishness.
> Do bear with me! [2]I feel a divine jealousy for you, for I
> betrothed you to Christ to present you as a pure bride
> to her one husband. [3]But I am afraid that as the serpent
> deceived Eve by his cunning, your thoughts will be
> led astray from a sincere and pure devotion to Christ.
> [4]For if some one comes and preaches another Jesus
> than the one we preached, or if you receive a different
> spirit from the one you received, or if you accept a different gospel from the one you accepted, you submit
> to it readily enough.

The opening to this chapter penetrates the heart of the concern Paul has with regard to the "super apostles" who are trying to usurp his place. They have changed the very nature of the Gospel itself, and they present "another Jesus" and a "different spirit." Their emphasis on success distorts the true Gospel of Jesus Christ crucified. They deny the role suffering has in the life of the Christian, allowing us to be united with Christ's suffering in order to be united with His comfort. They change the understanding of Jesus' fulfilling the role of the suffering servant Who dies for everyone's salvation and Who summons each of us to share in the same role as suffering servants. In effect, this defense is not just about Paul; it concerns the very core of the gospel and the essential relationship we all must have with the true Jesus Christ.

Over the centuries various people have claimed to have new gospels, Christs, and spirits. The same is true today. One popular version is the so-called "prosperity gospel," made famous by televangelists, which links worldly success, particularly financial prosperity, with God's blessing and favor.

Note Paul's fear that the Corinthians have accepted a different Christ, a different gospel, and a different Holy Spirit. He understands and explains this with two images. First, he compares himself to a matchmaker who has betrothed the Church to Christ. This is the earliest mention in the New Testament of an image of the Church as the Bride of Christ; Paul will develop this theme more extensively in Ephesians 5. Second, he goes back to the story of the Fall in Eden as a model for understanding how a Church/Bride might slip into sin through a temptation. For the Corinthians, the temptation appears in the guise of the "super apostles," transforming themselves as easily as Satan, who can appear as an angel of light (see 11:13–14).

B. 2 Corinthians 11:23–12:5

Stop here and read the text in your own Bible.

This section of the text presents Paul's claim to be a servant of Christ. However, notice that the repeated theme of his service is his own suffering. One would expect Paul to answer the claims of spiritual powers made by the "super apostles" with his own list of miracles and wonders — which, based on Acts of the Apostles, would be reasonably easy for him to do. However, Paul focuses on a long list of suffering and persecution for Christ as his credentials.

He then summarizes his boasting of his weakness rather than strength, adding one more event from the time of his first conversion in Damascus. This demonstrates that weakness has characterized his Christian life from its very inception.

Paul touches off his autobiographical section with a mention of his visions and revelations, going back to the early 40s A.D. He boasted about these experiences because the "super apostles" had apparently been claiming to have such visions, too. They considered themselves superior to Paul in this regard, *so* he trumps their claims with a report of his own visions. However, note that the wondrous experience of these visions leads directly to the next section, which presents the most profound theology of Christian suffering. Though the visions were an amazing gift, Paul could also see the danger of becoming filled with pride, much the way the "super apostles" had become. However, it was the Lord, not Paul, who popped an inflated ego with a thorn in the flesh.

> *i* Since 2 Corinthians was written around A.D. 55 or 56, then these visions occurred in A.D. 41 or 42. This probably belongs to the period when he is still living at Tarsus, or had recently come to Antioch.

INVESTIGATE

In 2 Corinthians 11:21–22, Paul presents his ethnic credentials. Note that he does not call himself a "Jew" here, but rather an Israelite and a Hebrew. In fact, Paul was not Jewish. "Jew" was the designation of an Israelite from the tribe of Judah. Paul was from the tribe of Benjamin; hence, he was a Benjaminite.

Read Genesis 35:23–26 and list the twelve tribes of Israel.

Today, the word "Jew" includes both those who consider themselves Jewish because of their religion and those who claim Jewish ancestry—even though they may be atheistic, agnostic, or nonpracticing, or have converted to Christianity or other religions. Vatican II (*Lumen Gentium*, n. 16) says that the Jewish people are "most dear for the sake of the Father for the gifts of God are without repentance."

STUDY

A. 2 Corinthians 12:6–10

> 6Though if I wish to boast, I shall not be a fool, for I shall
> be speaking the truth. But I refrain from it, so that no
> one may think more of me than he sees in me or hears
> from me. 7And to keep me from being too elated by
> the abundance of revelations, a thorn was given me in
> the flesh, a messenger of Satan, to harass me, to keep
> me from being too elated. 8Three times I besought the
> Lord about this, that it should leave me; 9but he said
> to me, "My grace is sufficient for you, for my power is
> made perfect in weakness." I will all the more gladly
> boast of my weaknesses, that the power of Christ may
> rest upon me. 10For the sake of Christ, then, I am con-
> tent with weaknesses, insults, hardships, persecutions,
> and calamities; for when I am weak, then I am strong.

Second Corinthians includes three descriptions of Paul's sufferings. Having finished the last of these, Paul now describes his theology of suffering. Keeping in mind his defense against the "super apostles," his main point is that his suffering is neither an indication of his insufficiency as an apostle nor is it absurd. Rather, it has tremendous meaning and power in light of Christ's Cross.

Paul did not enjoy or desire the thorn in his flesh. He petitioned Our Lord to remove it, but was denied. Yet, it is precisely in this state of Paul's weakness that the Lord manifests His strength. The same is often true for the thorns of many Christians. The task for us is to discover the ways in which Christ's grace becomes perfect in our weakness. One may never enjoy the weakness, but the servant of the Lord learns how Christ uses it to manifest His power.

B. 2 Corinthians 12:19–21

> 19Have you been thinking all along that we have been defending ourselves before you? It is in the sight of God that we have been speaking in Christ, and all for your
> upbuilding, beloved. 20For I fear that perhaps I may come and find you not what I wish, and that you may find me not what you wish; that perhaps there may be quarreling, jealousy, anger, selfishness, slander, gossip,
> conceit, and disorder. 21I fear that when I come again my God may humble me before you, and I may have to mourn over many of those who sinned before and have not repented of the impurity, immorality, and licentiousness which they have practiced.

Paul now explains his real purpose in writing: he is not simply defending himself to the Corinthians; he is building them up in Christ. The warning that they might not meet his expectations, nor he theirs, is akin to a mother saying, "Wait until your father gets home!" He threatens to correct the desires and works of the flesh. However, the warning here is a way to admonish them to change their ways before he arrives.

C. 2 Corinthians 13:1–9

> 1This is the third time I am coming to you. Any charge must be sustained by the evidence of two or three wit-
> nesses. 2I warned those who sinned before and all the others, and I warn them now while absent, as I did when present on my second visit, that if I come again I will
> not spare them — 3since you desire proof that Christ is speaking in me. He is not weak in dealing with you, but
> is powerful in you. 4For he was crucified in weakness,

> but lives by the power of God. For we are weak in him,
> but in dealing with you we shall live with him by the
> power of God.
>
> 5Examine yourselves, to see whether you are holding to
> your faith. Test yourselves. Do you not realize that Jesus
> Christ is in you? — unless indeed you fail to meet the
> test! 6I hope you will find out that we have not failed.
> 7But we pray God that you may not do wrong — not
> that we may appear to have met the test, but that you
> may do what is right, though we may seem to have failed.
> 8For we cannot do anything against the truth, but only
> for the truth. 9For we are glad when we are weak and
> you are strong. What we pray for is your improvement.

Paul now turns the tables on the Corinthians, who have been judging him unfavorably in comparison to the "super apostles." At this point in the letter, he is the judge of the Corinthians. His upcoming third visit, along with the previous two visits, will act as witnesses against them. His proof that Christ is truly speaking in him, rather than in the "super apostles," is that Christ had become weak by being crucified. Paul's whole point in describing his weakness is to show his identification with Christ's weakness on the Cross. He has completely united with Christ crucified, unlike the "super apostles," who claim great power. Paul asserts that the "super apostles" changed the gospel, changed Christ, and changed the Spirit (11:4); Paul, on the other hand, lives and preaches the same Christ who died as a sin offering for sinners in need of reconciliation with God.

Paul concludes his discussion with a request for a double examination of conscience. First, to test to see whether Jesus Christ — the true Jesus — is within them. This will be seen in their own conformity with Christ crucified, as Paul himself is so conformed. Second, to examine their own compliance with the truth about Christ and morality. That will be their true strength and the goal of Paul's prayer and exhortation throughout this entire epistle.

> "The grace of the Lord Jesus Christ and the love of God and the fellowship of the Holy Spirit be with you all."

The above concluding line of 2 Corinthians 13:14 is familiar to us from the Mass. Pope John Paul II consciously used this verse to structure much of his teaching during his pontificate. He taught about the Trinity in three encyclicals: *Redemptor Hominis* (*The Redeemer of Man*), which is on Christ; *Dives in Misericordia* (*God Who Is Rich in Mercy*), which is on God the Father; and *Dominum et Vivificantem* (*The Lord and Giver of Life*), which is on the Holy Spirit.

Pope John Paul II also organized the three years of preparation for the A.D. 2000 Jubilee of the Incarnation in the same manner, dedicating a year to Jesus Christ, then to the Father, and, finally, to the Holy Spirit.

DISCUSS

1. How does Paul's concept of the Body of Christ help you understand how your suffering can benefit the entire Church?

2. In light of the idea that we must die to self before we can rise with Christ, in what ways is your daily life both a dying and a rising in Christ?

3. Jesus said to take up our cross and follow Him. What is your cross? Are you resisting it or accepting it? How can you accept it more graciously?

4. Why do you think Paul spends so much time talking about his own suffering? Do you think it's right to talk about your suffering or should you "suffer in silence"?

5. What is the difference between accepting suffering and being a masochist?

PRACTICE

Use the problems listed in 2 Corinthians 12:20–21 as an examination of conscience before going to the Sacrament of Reconciliation (Confession).

Session Three

SAVED BY THE CROSS

Galatians

CONSIDER

Paul's letter to the growing faith community in the Roman province of Galatia contains some of his key teachings on the significance of the Law in relation to the gospel of faith in Christ Jesus. This includes discussions of the curse of being crucified and an important answer to it, as well as Paul's own recognition of the need to be crucified with Christ. This epistle serves as an important explanation of the theme of the Cross in Paul's teaching.

ⓘ This letter of Paul was addressed to the residents of the Roman province of Galatia, most likely the cities Perge, Iconium, Pisidian Antioch, Lystra, and Derbe, located in modern-day Turkey (Acts 13:13–14:27). Paul visited the area on his second and third journeys.

STUDY

A. Galatians 1:1–5

1Paul, an apostle — not from men nor through man, but
through Jesus Christ and God the Father, who raised

> him from the dead — [2]and all the brethren who are
> with me, To the churches of Galatia: [3]Grace to you and
> peace from God the Father and our Lord Jesus Christ,
> [4]who gave himself for our sins to deliver us from the
> present evil age, according to the will of our God and
> Father; [5]to whom be the glory for ever and ever. Amen.

Paul begins by calling himself an "apostle," one who is chosen by God to fulfill this role. The Church did not choose him, since a vocation is not bestowed by other people. God alone called him. Of special note is Paul's statement that "grace and peace" come from God the Father and our Lord Jesus, indicating that God and Jesus are equal sources of grace and peace. At the same time, the expression "giving himself up" refers to Christ's death. Grace and peace flow from the fact that Jesus willingly gave Himself up according to the Father's will to "deliver us from the present evil age."

> *i* Greeks greeted each other with the word "grace" while the Jews greeted each other with the word "peace." Saying "Grace to you and peace" indicates Paul is addressing a community composed of both Gentiles and Jews.

B. Galatians 1:6–12

> [6]I am astonished that you are so quickly deserting him
> who called you in the grace of Christ and turning to a
> different gospel — [7]not that there is another gospel, but
> there are some who trouble you and want to pervert
> the gospel of Christ. [8]But even if we, or an angel from
> heaven, should preach to you a gospel contrary to that

> which we preached to you, let him be accursed. [9]As
> we have said before, so now I say again, If any one is
> preaching to you a gospel contrary to that which you
> received, let him be accursed. [10]Am I now seeking the
> favor of men, or of God? Or am I trying to please men?
> If I were still pleasing men, I should not be a servant of
> Christ. [11]For I would have you know, brethren, that the
> gospel which was preached by me is not man's gospel.
> [12]For I did not receive it from man, nor was I taught it,
> but it came through a revelation of Jesus Christ.

Similar to the warning against other gospels, another Jesus, or another Spirit in 2 Corinthians, Paul warns the Galatians against another gospel other than the one originally presented. He says to be wary even if Paul himself, his companions, or an angel teach a new gospel. Such a gospel is false and a perversion of the authentic gospel, which is centered on the death and Resurrection of Jesus and the power of the Cross. The gospel that Paul had already delivered was given to him by Jesus Christ, and it did not come from any human source. Therefore, any change in the gospel will falsify it because it contradicts what Jesus has revealed.

> *i* The term "Judaizer" usually refers to a group of people who believed that all Gentiles who became Christian must first become Jews. This issue lies at the heart of the first Church Council, the Council of Jerusalem, which is recalled in Acts 15.

C. Galatians 1:13–2:14, Paul's Autobiographical Material

This autobiographical section contains important information about Paul's life, but he gives this information in order to strengthen his theological points. In this section, Paul wants to demonstrate from his own experience, particularly in relation to the leaders from Jerusalem, that the attempts to force the Gentile converts to take on Jewish practices such as circumcision were contrary to the normal ways of proceeding that had already been established in the Church, as well as to the message of the Cross that Paul himself taught. In other words, Paul wants to show that Gentiles did not have to follow the Laws of the Torah before becoming Christians.

INVESTIGATE

Read the following passages and answer the questions.

Galatians 1:13. What was Saul's original attitude toward the Church?

Galatians 1:14. What was Saul's attitude toward his Judaism? Did he seem satisfied with it or not?

Galatians 1:15–17. Give the key elements he uses in describing his conversion, especially in regard to his basic theology.

____

____

____

Galatians 1:18–24. Connect Paul's earliest relations with the members of the Church to his claim to the authority of the gospel in Galatians 1:12.

____

____

____

Galatians 2:1–3. What was Paul's relationship to leaders of the Church after his first fourteen years as a Christian? Pay attention to those elements related to his issues of confronting the Judaizers in the Galatian community.

____

____

____

Galatians 2:4–5. Who were his opponents in Jerusalem and what does he think of them? These, by the way, were the Judaizers.

Galatians 2:6–10. In contrast to the Judaizers, what attitude did the leaders take to Paul and his gospel?

Galatians 2:11–14. How does Paul treat Cephas (Peter) when the Judaizers pressure him to separate himself from the Gentile Christians?

STUDY

A. Galatians 2:15–17

> 15We ourselves, who are Jews by birth and not Gentile sinners, 16yet who know that a man is not justified by works of the law but through faith in Jesus Christ, even we have believed in Christ Jesus, in order to be justified by faith in Christ, and not by works of the law, because by works of the law shall no one be justified.
>
> 17But if, in our endeavor to be justified in Christ, we ourselves were found to be sinners, is Christ then an agent of sin? Certainly not!

Having given some elements of his own life that support his position, Paul sets forth the main lines of his argument against the Judaizing faction who had come to Galatia. Based on the ways he tries to contradict them, we can deduce that they were telling the baptized Galatians that they needed to have their men circumcised in order to be genuine Christians. He will identify circumcision as a "work of the Law" that cannot justify a person. Rather, justification is by faith in Jesus Christ, who was crucified to redeem the human race.

Paul begins this section by bringing up the points of agreement with the Judaizers, signaled by the phrase "we ourselves know." He believes that he and his opponents share the belief that people are justified by faith in Jesus Christ rather than by works of the Law.

The word "justified" refers to being declared right or innocent in a court of law. Israelite courts did not declare a person guilty or not guilty; rather, the verdict would be delivered as "wicked," "evil," or "righteous" (see Exodus 23:6–8 for an example). Here Paul assumes that the judge is God, who determines the norms of being right. Human beings need to correspond to his righteousness.

WHAT IS "THE LAW"?

In the Hellenistic period (fourth through first centuries B.C.), the first five books of the Bible came to be known as "the Law," although the Hebrew name, "Torah," means "instruction," not "law." Though it does contain 613 laws, the majority of the material in the Torah is narratives of the world's and early Israel's history. It became identified with "the Law" when Jews asked to be exempt from many of the duties of Hellenistic citizens because they contradicted Jewish laws. When Greeks asked for the source of these laws, Jews could point to the Torah, which had been translated into Greek by the 250s B.C. Incidentally, these books are known in Greek as the Pentateuch, which means "five scrolls." The word *teuchos* in Greek can mean a vessel or a container for scrolls.

However, Paul, like his opponents, knows that the "works of the law" cannot make even the Jews righteous, yet alone the Gentiles. Instead, it is "by faith in Jesus Christ that we are made righteous," i.e., proclaimed innocent of sin before God.

The final clause of verse 16 comes from Psalm 143:2, "For no man living is righteous before thee." In some translations, Paul reads the verse a little differently from the Hebrew or Greek version by saying "all flesh will not be righteous by works of the Law." His use of flesh rather than "every living being" may be related to his understanding of the term "flesh." Sometimes, this term simply refers to that which is human; other times, it refers to that which is sinful and corruptible in human beings. Paul may be trying to preserve this ambiguity in the text.

Finally, in verse 17, he agrees that if those who are justified by Christ are still found to be sinners, Christ is not causing them to sin. Apparently Paul's opponents accused him of saying that Christ is an "agent of sin," perhaps alleging that Paul blames Christ for continued sin in the believer.

INVESTIGATE

Paul says that trying to live by the Law is to live under a curse. In contrast, living by faith brings abundant life. Read the following passages and note the differences between living under the Law and living by faith.

PASSAGE	KEY CONCEPTS
Galatians 3:11–12	
Habakkuk 2:4	
Leviticus 18:5	
Galatians 3:19–29	

STUDY

The new Christians Paul is addressing in this Epistle were being pressured to add certain elements of Jewish law, such as circumcision, in order to assure salvation. By doing so, they were insinuating that Paul's gospel differed from that of the apostles in Jerusalem. His letter both defends his credentials and establishes the true basis of faith — the Cross of Christ.

He begins the letter with a long, personal defense, explaining how he came to understand the gospel, "For I did not receive it from man, nor was I taught it, but it came through a revelation of Jesus Christ" (Galatians 1:12).

He begins to get to the heart of his distress in chapter 2, when he explains that he confronted Cephas (Peter) for hypocrisy: "But when I saw that they were not on the right road in line with the truth of the gospel, I said to Cephas in front of all, "If you, though a Jew, are living like a Gentile and not like a Jew, how can you compel the Gentiles to live like Jews?" (Galatians 2:14, NABRE).

At the end of that chapter, he begins to delve into what will become his central theme for the rest of the letter: the power of the Cross.

A. Galatians 2:16–21

> 16Yet we know that a man is not justified by works of
> the law but through faith in Jesus Christ, even we have
> believed in Christ Jesus, in order to be justified by faith
> in Christ, and not by works of the law, because by works
> of the law shall no one be justified. 17But if, in our en-
> deavor to be justified in Christ, we ourselves were found
> to be sinners, is Christ then an agent of sin? Certainly
> not! 18But if I build up again those things which I tore
> down, then I prove myself a transgressor. 19For I through

> the law died to the law, that I might live to God. I have been crucified with Christ; [20]it is no longer I who live, but Christ who lives in me; and the life I now live in the flesh I live by faith in the Son of God, who loved me and gave himself for me. [21]I do not nullify the grace of God; for if justification were through the law, then Christ died to no purpose.

In this passage, Paul sets forth the main lines of his argument against the Judaizing faction who had come to Galatia. Justification is by faith in Jesus Christ crucified, not by works of the Law.

One of his key points is that "A person is not justified (*dikaioutai*) by works of the law."

Rather than the sense of being declared "right" in a court of law, it is "by faith in Jesus Christ that we are made righteous (*dikaiothomen*); all flesh will not be made righteous (*dikaiothesetai*) by the works of the law." This is a denial of the Pharisees' doctrine of righteousness by works of the Law. Doing works of the Jewish law will not make a person innocent before God's throne on the Day of Judgment; rather, faith in Jesus Christ is able to mediate the righteousness that every human needs in order to be saved. That is, Jesus is the Christ, the Messiah, whose death is able to save sinners. The final clause of this verse is Paul's interpretation of Psalm 143:2, "For no man living is righteous before thee." Paul adds that "all flesh will not be righteous by works of the law."

Being justified is something that takes place in Christ. Paul's opponents accused him of saying that it is Christ who is an "agent of sin." Their allegation is that Paul makes Christ to blame for continued sin in the believer. Paul gives his view of how one is made righteous by pointing to his own experience. "I have been crucified with Christ; it is no longer I who live, but Christ who lives in me; and the life I now live in the flesh I live by faith in the Son of God, who loved me and gave himself for me." The life of righteousness means being crucified with Christ. Obviously, this is not a literal experience of hanging on a cross, but a figure for some transformation of Paul's ego. This transformation takes place because of his faith rather than through obedience to the Torah.

The contrast that Paul makes is between grace and righteousness through the Law. If one chooses righteousness through obedience to the Torah, then both grace and the death of Christ are useless. Righteousness is either God's action in Christ's crucifixion and grace, or it is a human action of doing the Law. Paul wants the Galatians to give up their choice for the Law, as expressed in the requirement for circumcision. They are to heed his original gospel of grace and faith in Christ. In this text, "righteousness" (*dikaiosune*) describes what the act of making righteous is expected to produce in the believer: the state of righteousness before God.

Paul sets forth his arguments based on the Galatians' experience of receiving the Holy Spirit because of faith in Christ crucified, rather than through works of the Law.

B. Galatians 3:10–14

> 10For all who rely on works of the law are under a curse;
> for it is written, "Cursed be everyone who does not
> abide by all things written in the book of the law, and do
> them." 11Now it is evident that no man is justified before
> God by the law; for "He who through faith is righteous
> shall live"; 12but the law does not rest on faith, for "He
> who does them shall live by them." 13Christ redeemed
> us from the curse of the law, having become a curse
> for us — for it is written, "Cursed be everyone who
> hangs on a tree" — 14that in Christ Jesus the blessing

> of Abraham might come upon the Gentiles, that we might receive the promise of the Spirit through faith.

In these verses, Paul presents another contrast between the person who seeks to be righteous by observing the Torah versus one who relies on faith. He quotes from Habakkuk 2:4 to show that a righteous person lives by faith and from Leviticus 18:5 to show that the Law requires not faith, but obedience to its precepts. However, since it is impossible to perfectly keep all of the Law, one cannot live by doing the Law. Rather, one who tries to do the Law will receive the curses of the Law (v. 10).

Paul states here that God's action of making the Gentiles righteous is something that would take place by faith. This was not a message taught in the Old Testament, but Paul claims that it was foretold by Scripture in the promise of blessing that was given to Abraham. In 3:9, the act of being made righteous by God is now parallel to the "blessing." It is through the belief of Abraham that all of the nations would be blessed, according to the Torah (Genesis 12:3; 18:18; 22:18; 26:4; 28:1). Paul's logic is that since Abraham was "accounted as righteous" because he believed God's promise for a descendant (Genesis 15:6), and since Abraham is the person through whom all nations will be blessed, then the blessing must come to the nations by their own act of faith. This is not all of Paul's thought about this topic, but it is an important part of his thinking.

Christ on the Cross became a curse to free us from the curse of the law, so that the blessing of Abraham might be given to those who believe, and they might receive the Holy Spirit.

C. Galatians 6:14–17

> [14] But far be it from me to glory except in the cross of our Lord Jesus Christ, by which the world has been crucified to me, and I to the world.[15]For neither circumcision

counts for anything, nor uncircumcision, but a new
creation.[16]Peace and mercy be upon all who walk by
this rule, upon the Israel of God.

[17]Henceforth let no man trouble me; for I bear on my
body the marks of Jesus.

Paul boasts of the Cross of Jesus Christ, by whom the world is crucified to Paul and he to the world. This makes him a new creation (2 Corinthians 5:17), so much so that he even experiences the marks of Christ's Crucifixion in his own body. In verse 16, he wishes peace and mercy for those who walk according to this rule of boasting in the Cross of Christ.

THE STIGMATA

Stigmata is the plural of the Greek word *stigma*, meaning "mark" or "tattoo." For Christians, the stigmata are the wounds of Christ. Most often they appear in the hands, feet, and forehead, corresponding to the nail marks and crown of thorns. Three hundred or so individuals have received these marks over the centuries, as a sign of their physical participation in the suffering of Christ. Sts. Francis of Assisi and Padre Pio are the most famous recipients.

Lists of vices and virtues were common in the ancient world. What makes Paul's list different is that he stresses that the Spirit leads us to demonstrate the virtues, not mere adherence to the Law.

INVESTIGATE

Paul's letter to the Galatians provides us with both the major sins of the flesh and the fruits of the Spirit that have become available to us through the power of the Cross. Look up the following passages.

PASSAGE	SIN OR VIRTUE
Galatians 6:20	
Galatians 6:21	
Galatians 6:22	
Galatians 6:23	

DISCUSS

1. Which fruit of the Spirit do you demonstrate most frequently in your life? What one is most lacking?

2. What does "justification by faith" mean to you? If you were to speak to a non-Catholic, how would you explain the Catholic meaning versus the common Protestant definition?

3. How can you offer up your suffering in union with Christ? Does it make it harder or easier when you do so?

PRACTICE

This week, stretch your comfort zone by doing one thing that you don't think you can do, because you are a new person through the power of Christ crucified. Perhaps give up a bad habit, like smoking, or start a new positive one, like regular exercise.

Session Four

DYING WITH THE CROSS

Romans

CONSIDER

Paul did not establish the Church in Rome, as he did so many other churches. During his missionary travels, he longed to visit the Christians at Rome; unlike all his other letters, which were addressed to communities and individuals he already knew, he wrote his epistle to the Romans before he had ever met them.

The book of Romans is a letter of introduction. Paul had planned to visit Rome after the spring of A.D. 58. However, his arrest in Jerusalem led to a nearly two-year imprisonment in Caesarea Maritima. Only after a dangerous voyage in late A.D. 59 did he actually arrive in Rome. Acts of the Apostles ends by saying that Paul was under house arrest in Rome for two years, awaiting a trial that is never described.

In this letter, Paul introduces the Roman community to his gospel of salvation. He tends to be more systematic in the presentation because he is not answering a question, as in 1 Corinthians, nor responding to problems and opposition, as in 2 Corinthians and Galatians. Therefore understanding this letter does not entail reconstructing questions, objections, or opponents, as in the three preceding letters.

The issues related to Paul's teaching on the Cross in Romans are especially associated with the themes of the first eight chapters of the letter — "the Gospel [as] the power of God for salvation to every one who has faith, to the Jew first and also to the Greek" (Romans 1:16). The first three chapters set forth the problem: because all people, whether Jew or Gentile, are "under the power of sin" (3:9), they are incapable of obtaining God's justice and they deserve God's wrath. Yet God has revealed the good news that he desires to save all people from the wrath by justifying them by faith in Jesus Christ who died on a cross to redeem the world.

Caesarea Maritima was a harbor city built by Herod the Great between 25 and 13 B.C. The capital of Judea and the official residence of Pontius Pilate, it lies about halfway between the modern cities of Tel Aviv and Haifa. (Pilate had come to Jerusalem at the time of Jesus' death because it was the Feast of Passover.) At its height, Caesarea was home to nearly 125,000 people. Philip the Evangelist lived there (Acts 8:40), and Peter was sent there to baptize the centurion Cornelius (Acts 10). Peter also went there after being delivered from prison (Acts 12:19), and King Herod Agrippa died there, having been "eaten by worms" (Acts 12:19–23).

INVESTIGATE

Read Romans 1:18–3:19 and identify the passages that answer the following questions:

1. How have the Gentiles acted to deserve the wrath of God?

2. What have the Jews done wrong to deserve the wrath of God?

PASSAGE	ACTION	GENTILE OR JEW?

STUDY

A. Romans 3:20–26

> [20]For no human being will be justified in his sight by works of the law, since through the law comes knowledge of sin.
>
> [21]But now the righteousness of God has been mani-
> fested apart from law, although the law and the prophets
> bear witness to it, [22]the righteousness of God through
> faith in Jesus Christ for all who believe. For there is

> no distinction; [23]since all have sinned and fall short of the glory of God, [24]they are justified by his grace as a gift, through the redemption which is in Christ Jesus, [25]whom God put forward as an expiation by his blood, to be received by faith. This was to show God's righteousness, because in his divine forbearance he had passed over former sins; [26]it was to prove at the present time that he himself is righteous and that he justifies him who has faith in Jesus.

Having explained the core problem in the world — that Jews and Gentiles deserve God's wrath — Paul now explains that it is possible for people to be freely justified by God through the redemption that is in Christ Jesus. He calls this redemption an "expiation" by Christ's blood.

> *i* Frequently in the Old Testament — especially in Exodus, Leviticus, and Numbers — the term "expiation" refers to the gold-covered lid of the Ark of the Covenant. The high priest would sprinkle the blood of a bull and a goat on the lid on the Day of Atonement, the one day he was allowed to enter the Holy of Holies inside the Temple.

In Romans 3:25, the expiation by Christ's blood obviously refers to Christ's death on the Cross. Paul makes four main points:

First, Christ's blood of expiation is put forward by God. Thus it is an action by divine initiative rather than mere human endeavor.

Second, this offer of Christ's blood is called an "expiation," a term that refers to the sacrifice on the Day of Atonement. However, instead of the blood of bulls and goats, the blood of Jesus Christ is the expiation offered on Mt. Calvary on Good Friday.

DAY OF ATONEMENT — YOM KIPPUR

The Day of Atonement, or Yom Kippur, is the most solemn of the Jewish holy days. With Rosh Hashanah, it comprises the Jewish High Holy Days. The rituals in the Temple, which included sprinkling the blood of the goat as a sin offering for the people and the blood of a bull on the mercy seat (i.e., the *hilasterion*, or expiation) inside the Holy of Holies, were for the reparation of sin, as described in Leviticus 16, particularly v. 15. In Acts 27:9, it is called the "autumn fast" because the feast occurs in the fall and is a strict day of rest and fasting.

Third, our faith is the way we receive the forgiveness of sins that God offers us in Christ's blood. Humans cannot earn the redemption or the forgiveness of sins. Rather, faith in Christ and His redeeming blood is God's way to receive reconciliation.

Fourth, since access to the forgiveness of sins comes through faith in Jesus Christ's expiation, this forgiveness is available to everyone who has fallen short of the glory of God, both Gentiles and Jews. This makes the death of Jesus on Calvary quite distinct from the expiation sacrifices on the Day of Atonement. Those sacrifices could be offered only once a year by the high priest in the Holy of Holies for the forgiveness of Israel's sin. Christ's death just outside Jerusalem's gates, with Pontius Pilate's notification sign in Hebrew, Greek, and Latin, symbolizes the availability of the Cross to everyone who has ever sinned. Furthermore, this expiation is not merely offered once a year — it is offered once and for all.

INVESTIGATE

The concept of Christ the High Priest offering Himself as an expiation also appears in Hebrews—a letter that, according to the Greek Fathers of the Church and most modern scholars, is most likely not written by Paul (even though some older texts attribute it to him). Look up these passages that assert that Christ's death is once and for all.

PASSAGE	IMPORTANT POINTS
Hebrews 7:27	
Hebrews 9:7	
Hebrews 9:12	
Hebrews 9:26	

If Christ's death is once and for all, how is it that Paul says that every time Christians celebrate the Eucharist, they are proclaiming the death of the Lord (1 Corinthians 11:26)? Why is Mass repeated daily—multiple times daily—if Christ's death is once and for all?

The key to understanding this mystery is Christ's divine nature. He took on a complete human nature within the limits of time, yet He retains His full divine nature. This divine nature is truly eternal and timeless. In other words, God has neither past nor future, but only the present. Therefore, the death of Jesus remains present to His divine nature for all eternity. He never loses it to a past because God has no past, only the present. Because Jesus is God made man, He can make this eternal expiation available to each person who believes in Him — no matter when or where the person lives.

STUDY

Note: Romans 4 continues Paul's teaching on justification by faith along the lines he had developed in Galatians.

Romans 5:1–11

> [1]Therefore, having been made righteous by faith, we have peace with God through our Lord Jesus Christ, [2]through whom also we have had access by faith into this grace in which we stand. And we boast on the hope of the glory of God. [3]More than that, we rejoice in our sufferings, knowing that suffering produces endurance, [4]and endurance produces character, and character produces hope, [5]and hope does not disappoint us, because God's love has been poured into our hearts through the Holy Spirit which has been given to us.
>
> [6]Indeed, while we were weak, Christ died in due time for impious persons. [7]For barely on account of a righteous person will anyone die, though perhaps on account of a good person someone may dare to die. [8]But God shows His love to us in that while we were still sinners Christ died for us. [9]Therefore, by how much more now having been made righteous by His blood, shall we be saved through Him from the wrath.[10]For if while we were enemies we were reconciled to God by the death of his Son, much more, now that we are reconciled, shall we

> be saved by his life. [11]Not only so, but we also rejoice in God through our Lord Jesus Christ, through whom we have now received our reconciliation.
>
> *(author translation)*

In 5:1, Paul summarizes his teaching about being justified by grace and begins to discuss the effects of this justice on each of us.

First, this process of "having been made righteous" by faith is the prerequisite for having "peace with God through our Lord Jesus Christ." The term "righteousness" may mean the forensic declaration of innocence, which is made by an appeal to faith in Jesus Christ's death on the Cross, the shedding of His blood. "Righteousness" can also mean the moral rectitude by which a person's character and behavior conform to God's norms. Possibly Paul wants both ideas to apply here as the prerequisite for peace with God.

Second, this is a peace with God, the source of our existence who is also our goal and purpose of existence. That is the reason for hope of God's glory (5:2). Glory is associated with God's presence in the Temple, and therefore with His presence in Heaven, which is the eternal temple for which the earthly temple is merely a model.

In 5:3–5, Paul develops the concept of hope by "boasting" (a more literal translation than "rejoicing") in his tribulations, much as he had done in earlier letters.

He knows that his tribulation leads to patience, which develops tested virtue, which, in turn, produces hope (5:3–4). This hope does not disappoint the high expectations we have for eternal life in the presence of God's glory because it is based on the love that God has poured out in our hearts through the Holy Spirit (5:5). Therefore, the person who has confidence in God will not be able to be disappointed.

Paul goes on to say that we have already been made righteous by the blood of Christ because God so loves us, even while we are sinners, that His Son, Jesus, died for us. If God were willing to do this when we were so bad, then we can have a deep conviction that we will be saved.

This text shows that God's love is far superior to any love we can hope for, since it depends purely on God's gracious concern to redeem us from sin. It also indicates that God's love involves all three persons of the Trinity: the love of God is poured into our hearts through the Holy Spirit (5:5), and is proven by God the Father letting Christ His Son die for us sinners (5:8).

However, Paul still looks forward to being saved by Jesus' life. He refers to both the life that comes from Jesus' Resurrection and the future hope of being saved, which has not yet happened. Paul believes that by the sacrifice of Jesus on the Cross, his sins were forgiven and he was reconciled to God, but he does not yet have an absolute assurance that he has already been saved. Rather, he will tell the Philippians to "work out your own salvation with fear and trembling" (Philippians 2:12). It is only after Christ has issued His final judgment on our lives that we can say with absolute confidence that we have been saved.

Nevertheless, this does not mean that Paul — and by extension the rest of us — should be bound up with doubt and despair. Paul is confident that he shall be saved from God's wrath, a confidence that gives him freedom to hope for God's glory. As anyone who has ever gotten out of a deserved punishment knows, this is reason for rejoicing.

Paul's basis for hope is that if God loves sinners so much that He sent Jesus Christ to die for them and to make them righteous by means of the Blood that Jesus shed on the Cross, then we can be sure that at the last judgment we who have been made righteous will be saved from the wrath of God. In other words, having been made righteous is a preparation for being saved on the Day of Judgment.

Stop here and read Romans 5:12–21.

Although this section of Romans does not explicitly mention Christ's death on the Cross, it forms an important bridge to the next sections of the letter, which do. The main point is that all have sinned because everyone is a descendant of the first Adam: all must die as punishment for sin. However, Christ is the second Adam, who forgives sin and restores righteousness and life more abundantly. Paul makes it clear that Adam and Christ are not equal; Christ is far superior to Adam (5:15–17). While the single offense of Adam led to death for all of his descendants, through Christ's single act of redemption on the Cross will come grace, righteousness, and the possibility of eternal life.

INVESTIGATE

Look up these passages where the glory of the Lord appears in the Pentateuch. Note which of these passages show that God appears to humans in glory. Note also the passages where the glory of God is closely connected with God's punishment of sinners.

PASSAGE	OCCURRENCE
Exodus 14:4, 17–18	
Exodus 24:15–18	

PASSAGE	OCCURRENCE
Exodus 33:18–23	
Exodus 40:33–35	
Leviticus 9:6, 23	
Numbers 14:10	
Numbers 16:19, 42	
Numbers 20:6	
Deuteronomy 5:24	

STUDY

A. Romans 6:1–14

[1]What shall we say then? Are we to continue in sin that
grace may abound? [2]By no means! How can we who
died to sin still live in it? [3]Do you not know that all of us
who have been baptized into Christ Jesus were baptized
into his death? [4]We were buried therefore with him by
baptism into death, so that as Christ was raised from
the dead by the glory of the Father, we too might walk
in newness of life.

[5]For if we have been united with him in a death like his,
we shall certainly be united with him in a resurrection
like his. [6]We know that our old self was crucified with
him so that the sinful body might be destroyed, and we
might no longer be enslaved to sin. [7]For he who has died
is freed from sin. [8]But if we have died with Christ, we
believe that we shall also live with him. [9]For we know
that Christ being raised from the dead will never die
again; death no longer has dominion over him. [10]The
death he died he died to sin, once for all, but the life
he lives he lives to God. [11]So you also must consider
yourselves dead to sin and alive to God in Christ Jesus.

[12]Let not sin therefore reign in your mortal bodies, to
make you obey their passions. [13]Do not yield your
members to sin as instruments of wickedness, but yield
yourselves to God as men who have been brought from
death to life, and your members to God as instruments
of righteousness. [14]For sin will have no dominion over
you, since you are not under law but under grace.

For Paul, the death of Christ, along with the Resurrection, is the power that underlies Baptism. His main argument is to offer us the certainty that the power of Baptism into Christ's death will lead to a Resurrection and glory like His. Paul makes this point to refute any potential opponent who might accuse him of teaching people to sin more and break God's law so as to acquire more graces in so sinning.

Having established the power of the sacrament of Baptism, he then moves to the effect of Christ's death on the Cross to transform each individual's life on a daily basis. The "old self" refers to the "sinful body" that enslaves a person to sin. In modern language, this would refer to the addictions to sinful behavior that impede or even destroy a person's freedom to act. On one level, the choice of doing a particular good or evil deed remains open to a person. However, the deeper freedom is to choose to do what is good.

The ability to choose the good is somewhat impaired in all humans, simply by the fact the evil seems easier, it is often quite appealing at the outset, and may have good motives underlying it. However, the more a person sins in a particular area, the more difficult it becomes to choose the good. Ask any alcoholic or drug user how difficult it is to change. The wisdom of Twelve-Step programs is for the addict to realize his or her inability to control the substance, to realize that a "higher power" is stronger than the substance, and ask the higher power to take charge of his or her life.

However, this passage from Paul goes far beyond an undefined higher power. Paul teaches that God allowed His Son to die on a cross and then rise again. The power to transform a sinner's life is not a vague theory, but the painful reality of the crucifixion of God the Son. His death puts our compulsive sinful parts to death. Thus, we are freed from sins we have already committed; because Christ is raised from the dead, never to die again, we, too, can have access to an ongoing power to live with the freedom to do what is good and right.

The ability to make the choices each day regarding each member of the body requires that the old self, the compulsively sinful self, be crucified with Jesus. If we do not tap into the power of Christ's death to die to ourselves, we will continue to obey the passions of sin. These passions will control us to a point of true spiritual death. The irony here is that dying to ourselves, through a deeper union with the Person of Jesus, means that we become more alive in grace. Precisely by submitting to grace, we become more free for goodness — more alive.

Earlier in this epistle, Paul presented the general principle that one receives grace and righteousness through faith in the saving and expiating death of Jesus Christ. However, he did not explain how one receives that grace except to say that it is by faith. In this section of the letter, he mentions Baptism as the instrument of grace.

Baptism is so powerful that the baptized person enters into the death and the Resurrection of Jesus Christ. The old human nature is crucified with Jesus in Baptism so that a person no longer serves sin, which leads to death (6:6). Paul explains that the person who has died to this old human nature has been made righteous (6:7).

Verses 6:12–14 use an image from the gladiatorial games. The choice is to use the members of one's body either as instruments of wickedness or as instruments of righteousness. The term "instrument" is a generic translation for a word commonly understood as "weapon," which makes better sense when we see the image of gladiators at work here. Human beings make choices in their minds and consciences. However, they actually accomplish good deeds or evil ones through the various members of their bodies. In that sense, these members are weapons to spread the power of evil or the power of righteousness.

i While we often think about the early Christian martyrs being thrown to the beasts in the Colosseum, that image is probably inaccurate. The earliest histories cite the Circus Flaminius as the site of martyrdoms, and most scholars today believe that few Christians were actually put to death in the Colosseum. Gladiatorial fights, mock battles, and the execution of political criminals were the most common occurrences in the Colosseum.

Paul exhorts the baptized Christians of Rome to not allow sin to reign in their mortal bodies through lusts and unrighteous deeds. This exhortation implies that the Christian still has the potential to choose such things, but also has the freedom of will to avoid them. Another implication of this text is that the Christian is engaged in a spiritual war. The weapons are the very members of the body that has experienced the power of Christ's death and Resurrection through Baptism. The transformation of the person is so total that the very members of one's body can be used to further the cause of righteousness. This also implies that righteousness is something that can increase in the world by means of the baptized Christian.

Notice that Paul speaks here about grace rather than about faith. He is concerned with the power that the transformed Christian has from God in order to serve God rather than the means by which the Christian receives that power (i.e., faith).

B. Romans 8:1–13

> 1There is therefore now no condemnation for those
> who are in Christ Jesus. 2For the law of the Spirit of
> life in Christ Jesus has set me free from the law of sin
> and death. 3For God has done what the law, weakened
> by the flesh, could not do: sending his own Son in the
> likeness of sinful flesh and for sin, he condemned sin
> in the flesh, 4in order that the just requirement of the

law might be fulfilled in us, who walk not according to the flesh but according to the Spirit.

[[3b]God sent His own Son in the likeness of a flesh of sin
and concerning sin, He condemned sin in the flesh, [4]in
order that the ordinance [*dikaioma*] of the law may be
fulfilled in us who do not walk according to the flesh
but according to spirit.]*

[5]For those who live according to the flesh set their
minds on the things of the flesh, but those who live
according to the Spirit set their minds on the things of
the Spirit. [6]To set the mind on the flesh is death, but
to set the mind on the Spirit is life and peace. [7]For the
mind that is set on the flesh is hostile to God; it does
not submit to God's law, indeed it cannot; [8]and those
who are in the flesh cannot please God.

[9]But you are not in the flesh, you are in the Spirit, if the
Spirit of God really dwells in you. Any one who does not
have the Spirit of Christ does not belong to him. [10]But
if Christ is in you, the body is dead because of sin but
the spirit is life because of righteousness (*dikaiosune*).*

[11]If the Spirit of him who raised Jesus from the dead
dwells in you, he who raised Christ Jesus from the dead
will give life to your mortal bodies also through his
Spirit which dwells in you.

[12]So then, brethren, we are debtors, not to the flesh, to
live according to the flesh — [13]for if you live according
to the flesh you will die, but if by the Spirit you put to
death the deeds of the body you will live.

* *(author translation)*

Note: In Romans 7, Paul returns to the theme of the law, where his discussion becomes more personal, focusing on his personal experience of trying to obey the Law of God with all his might, and yet finding himself unable to do so.

The beginning of Romans 8 is the response to the dilemma of the preceding chapter: the Holy Spirit overcomes the weakness of the flesh in order to set us free from the power of sin and guilt. However, this cannot be achieved apart from Christ's death on the Cross.

Anyone who has tried to diet, break a vice, become more patient, or stop a drug or alcohol habit knows the difficulty in changing old patterns of sin that make Paul's words — "There is therefore now no condemnation!" — so amazing. The key is that God has acted to redeem sinners when they have found themselves too weak to be good because of the flesh.

Paul explains that God sent the Son to take on the likeness of human flesh and its tendency toward sin in order to condemn that sin. This condemnation of sin in the flesh occurs by Jesus' death on the Cross, which makes possible the fulfillment of precepts of the Law by those who walk according to the Spirit (Romans 8:3–4). The significance of this understanding of Christ's Crucifixion helps us understand the next steps in the Christian life. While Paul has earlier addressed the role of saving faith in Christ's Cross and the connection of Baptism to the Cross and Resurrection, here he explains the link between the Cross and ongoing life in the Spirit. The Christian cannot continue to live according to God's law and the way of righteousness unless there is an ongoing experience of dying to the flesh in order to live by the Spirit of Jesus Christ.

Paul's point is to show that life in the Spirit must be a continuous rejection of the flesh. Both as a warning and as a way to inform the reader on how to discern between the flesh and the Spirit, Paul delineates some of their chief traits.

The flesh leads to death, hostility to God, the inability to submit to God's law, and the inability to please God. Committing oneself to the Spirit of Jesus Christ brings life and peace through righteousness and belonging to God. Each of us who has faith in the power of Christ's death will shift from commitment to the flesh to commitment to the life of the Spirit.

In addition, by living out this commitment to Christ, the promise of the resurrection from the dead is possible. However, this must be a continuous process of putting to death the deeds of the sinful flesh. Therefore, one must daily be joined to Christ's death on the Cross in order to effectively die to the flesh and live by the Spirit.

C. Romans 8:14–23

> [14]For all who are led by the Spirit of God are sons of
> God. [15]For you did not receive the spirit of slavery to
> fall back into fear, but you have received the spirit of
> sonship. When we cry, "Abba! Father!" [16]it is the Spirit
> himself bearing witness with our spirit that we are chil-
> dren of God, [17]and if children, then heirs, heirs of God
> and fellow heirs with Christ, provided we suffer with
> him in order that we may also be glorified with him.
>
> [18]I consider that the sufferings of this present time are
> not worth comparing with the glory that is to be re-
> vealed to us. [19]For the creation waits with eager longing
> for the revealing of the sons of God; [20]for the creation
> was subjected to futility, not of its own will but by the
> will of him who subjected it in hope; [21]because the cre-
> ation itself will be set free from its bondage to decay
> and obtain the glorious liberty of the children of God.
> [22]We know that the whole creation has been groaning

> in travail together until now; [23]and not only the creation, but we ourselves, who have the first fruits of the Spirit, groan inwardly as we wait for adoption as sons, the redemption of our bodies.

Paul begins this section by pointing out that we are in a new relationship with God: we are children, not slaves. Becoming God's children entails a number of factors.

First, we can call God "Father," even by the familiar Aramaic term *Abba.*

Second, as children, we become heirs with Christ. This means that we will inherit eternal life and the kingdom of God.

> The term for Father in Hebrew is *Ab*, a word that appears in many names, including Abraham ("father of a multitude"), and Eliab ("God of my father"). *Abba* is the word for "father" that is still used in Israel today. Jesus uses that precise word while praying in Gethsemane (Mark 14:36). It was extremely rare for rabbis to address God as "Abba," though a few Old Testament texts do. Christ not only instructed us to pray to God as "Our Father," but Paul indicates that it is the Holy Spirit who enables us to do so.

Third, we must suffer with Christ in order to receive the inheritance of being glorified with Him. As Paul had emphasized in 2 Corinthians, union with Christ includes suffering as Jesus did.

Paul continues with a serious consideration of "the sufferings of this present time" and speaks of "the creation being subject to futility" and "the whole creation groaning in travail." Just as he had looked back at Adam's sin and its subsequent deadly effects on the whole human race, so, now, he looks back to the effects on creation of man's sinful fall. Even though the sufferings of the present time are real, they are nothing compared to the glory we as children of God will inherit by virtue of having suffered with Christ. This union with Christ's suffering and death on the cross is connected to an "inward groaning" as we await our adoption, which Paul identifies as the redemption of our bodies. Therefore, we who share the Cross with Christ can also expect to share in His Resurrection from the dead.

INVESTIGATE

Look up these Old Testament texts that address God as Father:

PASSAGE	TITLE
Deuteronomy 32:6	
Isaiah 63:16	
Isaiah 64:8	
Jeremiah 3:19	

PASSAGE	TITLE
Jeremiah 31:9	
Malachi 1:6	
Malachi 2:10	

STUDY

Romans 8:24–25

> [24]For in this hope we were saved. Now hope that is seen
> is not hope. For who hopes for what he sees? [25]But if we
> hope for what we do not see, we wait for it with patience.

Paul now looks at the impact of the hope of our salvation. To understand its importance, consider life without anything to look forward to, that is, a life without hope. Roman religion could offer no hope for the afterlife and consequently no meaning to shame or pain in the present. Such lack of hope so dominated Roman culture that suicide was considered a noble response to public shame or defeat.

How many people today have reverted to this pagan perspective and choose suicide and euthanasia for themselves or others because they see no hope for the future? Their suffering in the present overwhelms them, and they befriend death as a way out of suffering in the present.

The success of prosperity in the modern world still cannot remove the "futility" of creation, and it cannot offer ultimately salvific hope.

In contrast, Paul teaches that we have a redemptive hope for the salvation of our bodies. This hope saves us partly because we can put the sufferings of the present life into a much wider perspective, namely, the hope of a far exceeding glory that God will reveal to us in Heaven and in the resurrection of our bodies from the dead.

True, we do not see this glory yet. If we saw it, then we would have present accomplishment rather than hope for the glory. However, we have the presence of the Holy Spirit within us — the "down payment" of the future glory.

INVESTIGATE

Paul talks about the Holy Spirit as a guarantee of the Christian life. The word he uses can be compared to a down payment on the future. How does that apply to the following verses?

PASSAGE	CONTENT
2 Corinthians 1:21–22	
2 Corinthians 5:4–5	
Ephesians 1:13–14	

STUDY

> Stop here and read Romans 7:14–19. What is the weakness that Paul sees in himself?

A. Romans 8:26–27

> 26 Likewise the Spirit helps us in our weakness; for we
> do not know how to pray as we ought, but the Spirit
> himself intercedes for us with sighs too deep for words.
> 27 And he who searches the hearts of men knows what
> is the mind of the Spirit, because the Spirit intercedes
> for the saints according to the will of God.

In these passages, Paul once again recognizes human weakness and its spiritual meaning.

> The precise term for "groaning" that Paul uses is not a description of the cries of Jesus on the Cross. However, three of the evangelists note these cries: Matthew 27:46–50; Mark 15:34–37; Luke 23:46 (John does not mention any crying out in 19:30).
>
> To see the connection between prayer and Jesus' cries on the Cross, read Psalm 22.

Here, our weakness includes the inability to know how to pray or even what to pray for. The common translation of 8:26 is "sighs," but the verbal root is translated as "groans." Sometimes people are so deeply caught in pain and suffering that all they can do at certain points of life is "groan" or "sigh." Paul's point is that the Holy Spirit who dwells within each of us is no further away from these painful groans than He was from the cries of pain of Jesus Christ on the Cross. In other words, the Holy Spirit can take up the groans and sighs we experience in our most difficult crises and make them into our prayer. With the Holy Spirit dwelling within us, God is never distant from our most painful cries and grief.

Another point is found in 8:27, where the implied subject is God the Father, who knows the mind of the Spirit. This is one of the rare instances where Paul speaks about the inner life of the Blessed Trinity. He wants to assure Christians about three distinct points regarding God: 1) the Holy Spirit is interceding for us; 2) the Father knows the mind of the Spirit; and 3) the Spirit will intercede only in a way in accord with the Father's will. From this we can have confidence that God knows our deepest and truest needs when we are at our lowest and most difficult points in life. No matter how abandoned we feel, no matter how little we think God understands the seriousness of our problems, our feelings do not reflect reality. Rather, as Jesus said, "your Father knows what you need before you ask him" (Matthew 6:8).

B. Romans 8:28–30

> 28We know that in everything God works for good with those who love him, who are called according to his purpose. 29For those whom he foreknew he also predestined to be conformed to the image of his Son, in order that he might be the firstborn among many brethren. 30And those whom he predestined he also called; and those whom he called he also justified; and those whom he justified he also glorified.

Paul's absolute confidence in God's providence flows from his teaching about the future renewal of creation. God's fatherly love will make the present pains and crises fade as He reveals the glory in store for those who have the hope that saves. In this section, the shift is toward the Christians. While it is God who has called us, it is we who must respond by loving God.

Love of God is not some warm feeling; in fact, it is not an emotion, though emotions may come into play. It is an act of the will, characterized by giving oneself to God. At the same time, love, along with faith and hope, is a theological virtue. This means that God bestows a gift of His grace that empowers one to love by giving oneself, just as the Father, the Son, and the Holy Spirit perpetually give themselves to each other within the life of the Trinity. Since such self-giving love is an act that belongs to God's very nature (1 John 4:7–8, "God is love"), it is clear that we need God's grace to be able to love in such a way. Nonetheless, we choose to accept this grace and we choose to return the love to God and to our fellow human beings.

Paul's point here is that those who choose to accept the grace of loving God can be confident that everything will turn out for their good. This does not mean that everything will be easy, satisfying, or painless, but it means that the calamities of life and death itself will be for our ultimate good.

C. Romans 8:31–39

> [31]What then shall we say to this? If God is for us, who
> is against us? [32]He who did not spare his own Son but
> gave him up for us all, will he not also give us all things
> with him? [33]Who shall bring any charge against God's
> elect? It is God who justifies; [34]who is to condemn?
> Is it Christ Jesus, who died, yes, who was raised from
> the dead, who is at the right hand of God, who indeed

> intercedes for us? [35]Who shall separate us from the love
> of Christ? Shall tribulation, or distress, or persecution,
> or famine, or nakedness, or peril, or sword? [36]As it is
> written, "For thy sake we are being killed all the day
> long; we are regarded as sheep to be slaughtered." [37]No,
> in all these things we are more than conquerors through
> him who loved us. [38]For I am sure that neither death,
> nor life, nor angels, nor principalities, nor things present,
> nor things to come, nor powers, [39]nor height, nor depth,
> nor anything else in all creation, will be able to separate
> us from the love of God in Christ Jesus our Lord.

Finally, this section of Romans 1–8 concludes with a proclamation of total faith and confidence that God is for us. He proves this by giving up his Son, even while we are still sinners. Even if someone tries to charge us with our past sins, we have confidence in God's love because it is God who justifies us (consider 3:20–5:1). Jesus Himself will not condemn us because He dies on the Cross for us, and even more powerfully, was raised from the dead and ascended to the Father's right hand to intercede for us. God is completely for us, and we need to have confidence in Him.

However, God's actions to save us do not remove us from the world and its sufferings. Rather, our confidence is so strong that we can be sure that no suffering endured in this life will ever separate us from the love of Christ. Rather, it is precisely in suffering that we are joined to Christ. We suffer with Him in order to be glorified with Him. Such is the power of the love of God and life in His Spirit.

DISCUSS

1. What are some of the sufferings you see in creation and human society?

2. What are some of the most difficult sufferings you have endured in your life?

   As you look back on that, how do you see those pains today? Have you changed your perspective on your sufferings because of any positive results that came from them?

3. Who are your favorite saints and why are you so attracted to them?

4. What were the trials and difficulties they endured? How did these events turn out to the good for these saints who loved God?

PRACTICE

A common practice used to be to "offer up" one's suffering. This week, when you find yourself complaining about something, instead, ask for God's grace to endure it and use it as a means to unite yourself with Christ for the salvation of others and the renewal of the world.

Session Five

CREATION AND THE CROSS

Philippians and Colossians

CONSIDER

These two letters of Paul contain many of the most poignant and moving passages written to the early Church. We are considering them together because the specific information relating to the importance and the power of the Cross is not as extensive as in his early writing, but still important enough that no examination of Paul's theology of the Cross would be complete without it.

Philippians

Paul wrote a very affectionate letter to the community at Philippi, indicating the close relationship he maintained with them over the years. Within this letter, he again addresses the central Christian theme of the Cross, and, as in 2 Corinthians and Galatians, we learn important autobiographical information about St. Paul. The first autobiographical information appears in 1:12–20, where he tells them that he is again in prison for Christ.

ⓘ Paul probably founded the first Christian Church in Europe at Philippi, in northeastern Greece. Named for Philip of Macedon, Alexander the Great's father, the city became Roman in the second century B.C. Paul wrote his letter to the Philippians when he was imprisoned and under danger of death.

Stop here and read Philippians 1:1–11 to see the way in which Paul expresses his love and concern for the Christians at Philippi.

STUDY

Philippians 1:21–30

We cannot be absolutely positive about which imprisonment Paul is discussing when he writes to the Philippians. However, the mention of a Praetorian guard indicates an important imperial city. Rome is one candidate, but Caesarea Philippi is more likely. This would place his letter between spring of A.D. 58 and late autumn of A.D. 59.

During this imprisonment, some rival Christians tried to make Paul's situation more difficult. Their apparent goal was to instigate worse treatment for Paul by making Christianity seem more contentious and perhaps even dangerous. Such action would make the charges against Paul look like a more serious threat to civil peace. However, Paul rejoices in their obnoxious behavior because he wants nothing better than to have Christ preached to more people. As far as he is concerned, life and death mean nothing in comparison to preaching the saving gospel of Jesus Christ.

> [27]Only let your manner of life be worthy of the gospel
> of Christ, so that whether I come and see you or am
> absent, I may hear of you that you stand firm in one
> spirit, with one mind striving side by side for the faith
> of the gospel, [28]and not frightened in anything by your
> opponents. This is a clear omen to them of their destruc-
> tion, but of your salvation, and that from God. [29]For it
> has been granted to you that for the sake of Christ you
> should not only believe in him but also suffer for his
> sake, [30]engaged in the same conflict which you saw and
> now hear to be mine.

In these verses, Paul now tries to explain his indifference to life and death. Death is "gain" because he has hope of being with Christ in Heaven. However, he sees that continued life is fruitful in helping the Philippians and the other Christians to progress in their faith. As it turns out, he believes that he will continue to live in this life in order to visit Philippi again and help them grow. Therefore, he gives some instruction on how to live until he returns to visit them. The first issue is to stand firm in their Christian unity. Second, he tells them to have no fear of their enemies, since that will be a sign of their coming destruction. Third, they are to accept the gift of suffering with Christ, just as they accept faith in Him. Such suffering with Christ is Paul's lot, and it belongs to all Christians, a point Paul consistently teaches.

INVESTIGATE

Which passages from the previous letters come to mind in regard to Paul's summons to suffer with Christ, whether from his own example or from his instruction to other Christians?

____

____

____

____

____

STUDY

A. Philippians 2:1–11

1So if there is any encouragement in Christ, any incen-
tive of love, any participation in the Spirit, any affection
and sympathy, 2complete my joy by being of the same
mind, having the same love, being in full accord and
of one mind. 3Do nothing from selfishness or conceit,
but in humility count others better than yourselves.
4Let each of you look not only to his own interests, but
also to the interests of others. 5Have this mind among
yourselves, which is yours in Christ Jesus, 6who, though
he was in the form of God, did not count equality with
God a thing to be grasped, 7but emptied himself, tak-
ing the form of a servant, being born in the likeness of
men. 8And being found in human form he humbled
himself and became obedient unto death, even death

> on a cross. 9Therefore God has highly exalted him and
> bestowed on him the name which is above every name,
> 10that at the name of Jesus every knee should bow, in
> heaven and on earth and under the earth, 11and every
> tongue confess that Jesus Christ is Lord, to the glory
> of God the Father.

Paul now returns to the call to unity, this time based on the community's love for Paul and on their participation in the Holy Spirit. He urges his readers to avoid selfishness by humbly treating others as their betters and by seeking others' best interests instead of their own concerns. Ultimately, this is a call to think like Jesus.

This exhortation to have the mind of Jesus introduces a hymn which portrays Christ as exemplifying this very humility and generosity. The hymn bears close examination, since it lies near the very core of St. Paul's theology of the Cross.

First, the hymn begins by assuming that Jesus existed before he became man. The question it poses concerns the nature of Jesus' existence prior to becoming man: Was His life before His human existence angelic, human, or otherwise?

Second, the hymn answers the question by saying that Jesus was in the form of God and not that of a human or an angel. Since God does not have an outward appearance perceivable by human senses, this term does not refer to some sort of physical shape. Rather, it means Jesus was God, as is confirmed by the phrase "equality with God."

Third, Jesus did not consider this equality with God something to be "grasped," which assumes that He already possessed the equality.

Fourth, Christ "emptied" Himself. This does not mean that He removed some divine quality but rather, it means He was "poured out." Christ pours Himself out generously, giving Himself completely. Such self-gift is at the very core of the God's nature as love (see 1 John 4:8,

"God is love"). This divine love is not an emotion or feeling of warmth, but a personal choice of the Father, the Son, and the Holy Spirit to give everything they have to each other in a perpetual and infinite pouring out of self. The hymn then recognizes that Christ pours Himself out to the creation in an act of self-gift.

Fifth, the verb "emptied" dominates the participles that follow, so as to demonstrate the way He empties Himself. His emptying comes by "taking the form of a servant" and being born in the likeness of men, recalling the servant songs of Isaiah, especially Isaiah 52:13–53:12.

> Stop here and read Isaiah 53:12. What are the verbal links between this part of Philippians and the verse in Isaiah?

Sixth, Christ's human form is directly connected with His humility and obedience unto death. The place where this obedience to the point of dying occurs is the Cross. This form of death — which was dreaded by everyone, Roman citizen and noncitizen alike — was inherently horrible. However, as noted earlier, death on a tree was considered accursed by the Old Testament in Deuteronomy 21:23: "For a hanged man is accursed by God." Therefore, the Cross was especially abhorrent to Jews, and Christ's sacrifice even more astonishing.

Seventh, after having described all that Jesus Christ had done, the hymn now turns to what God the Father did in response. The key is the exaltation of Christ the suffering servant, as had been predicted by Isaiah 52:13: "Behold, my servant shall prosper, he shall be exalted and lifted up, and shall be very high."

Eighth, since a name was understood to express the meaning or even essence of the object named, here the name that God gives to the servant is superior to every other name: Jesus Christ, the Lord. In this way, God reveals that Jesus has His equality with God manifested again after having been debased by suffering death on the Cross.

Ninth, in verses 10–11, the hymn concludes with a reference to Isaiah 45:22–23:

> [22]"Turn to me and be saved, all the ends of the earth! For I am God, and there is no other. [23]By myself I have sworn, from my mouth has gone forth in righteousness a word that shall not return: 'To me every knee shall bow, every tongue shall swear.'"

The context of these verses shows that only the Lord is God, and all creation — expressed by the all-inclusiveness of "in heaven, on earth, and under the earth" — will bow before the Lord God. However, the hymn proclaims that Jesus Christ is this Lord, and therefore identifies His glory as that of the Lord God made manifest after his Resurrection and Ascension into Heaven.

Tenth, the exaltation of Jesus after pouring Himself out to the point of death, and then being glorified as Lord, does not in any way compete with God the Father. Rather, His exaltation is directed solely to the glory of God the Father, and nothing less.

B. Philippians 2:12–17

> [12]Therefore, my beloved, as you have always obeyed, so
> now, not only as in my presence but much more in my
> absence, work out your own salvation with fear and
> trembling; [13]for God is at work in you, both to will and
> to work for his good pleasure. [14]Do all things without
> grumbling or questioning, [15]that you may be blameless
> and innocent, children of God without blemish in the
> midst of a crooked and perverse generation, among
> whom you shine as lights in the world, [16]holding fast

> the word of life, so that in the day of Christ I may be proud that I did not run in vain or labor in vain. [17]Even if I am to be poured as a libation upon the sacrificial offering of your faith, I am glad and rejoice with you all.

i We may not read these verses as a hymn, but scholars consider them as such because the Greek has a meter resembling other hymns in Greek. This meter cannot be reproduced in the English translation and is therefore missed by the reader. No one knows whether Paul composed this hymn or used someone else's hymn. Apparently that point was not important enough for anyone to have mentioned at the time.

Paul follows up the hymn with further exhortations to the community. The first is to obey him by working out their salvation in fear and trembling, while at the same time realizing that God is the one at work. Though God's grace is completely necessary, each Christian is actively involved in the process by cooperating with the grace. The reason for fear and trembling is not that God is untrustworthy, but that weak human beings might cease to cooperate. Therefore, we are to fear offending God by committing sin or by being presumptuous while, at the same time, working hard.

The second exhortation is to avoid grumbling and complaining about the evils in order to appear innocent in a corrupt and twisted world.

The third exhortation is to hold onto the word of God — presumably, that proclamation of the Gospel that Paul had delivered to them — in order to be proud of his labor as an evangelist on the day Christ returns to judge everyone. Directly connected to this desire for the judgment day is Paul's return to the theme of chapter 1, where he was unsure about whether he would live or be killed as a martyr. Paul sees his imprisonment and possible martyrdom as a "libation upon the sacrificial offering of your faith." A libation refers to the pouring out of wine along with a sacrifice. In this context, it is an image for Paul pouring out his own blood as a martyr for the sake of the Gospel, something he would do around A.D. 66 or 67. What is key here is to note that Paul understands his coming martyrdom as a sacrifice, just as he interpreted Christ's death as a sacrifice in Romans 3:25 and other passages.

INVESTIGATE

Libations appear in a few Old Testament passages. Look up the following passages and note the negative qualities. Can you connect those problems with the possibility of Paul being martyred?

PASSAGE	NEGATIVE QUALITIES
2 Kings 16:10–13	
Jeremiah 7:18	
Hosea 9:4	

CONSIDER

Colossians

This short letter to the Colossians is very tightly written to communicate a rich theology. It is addressed to the citizens of Colossae, which is located east of Ephesus in modern-day Turkey. The church had apparently been established by Epaphras of Colossae, who contacted Paul after certain problems concerning Christ's relation to the universe had arisen — issues quite different from the issues that had arisen in Paul's other communities. We will focus on the passages that present the Cross and its application to some of the local problems.

STUDY

A. Colossians 1:13–18

> 13He has delivered us from the dominion of darkness
> and transferred us to the kingdom of his beloved Son,
> 14in whom we have redemption, the forgiveness of sins.
>
> 15He is the image of the invisible God, the firstborn of all
> creation; 16for in him all things were created, in heaven
> and on earth, visible and invisible, whether thrones or
> dominions or principalities or authorities — all things
> were created through him and for him. 17He is before
> all things, and in him all things hold together. 18He is
> the head of the body, the church; he is the beginning,
> the firstborn from the dead, that in everything he might
> be preeminent.

The first part of this passage is a hymn to Christ and His power to redeem humanity and even the whole cosmos. The opening verses present the primary issue at stake in the redemption: humans exist within the dominion of darkness because they commit sin. Jesus redeems us by offering the forgiveness of sin and a consequent transfer from the dominion of darkness into the Kingdom of Christ, God's beloved Son. The rest of the hymn describes Christ's credentials, by which He is empowered to effect the forgiveness of sins and gain our entrance into His Kingdom.

Stop here and read John 1:1–18 and note the similarities between Paul's and John's descriptions.

Paul first identifies Christ here as the image of the invisible God. The Greek word for "image" is *icon.* By using this word, Paul means that Jesus is able to make the invisible God visible. This idea is similar to John's calling Christ the "Word" in John 1. A word makes known through the ears what is in the speaker's mind, just as an icon gives a picture for the eyes of what is in the painter's mind. The idea that Christ is the icon who makes God visible connects well with the last verse of St. John's prologue:

> No one has ever seen God; the only Son, who is in the bosom of the Father, he has made him known. — John 1:18

At the same time that Christ is the image of God, He is also the firstborn of all creation. Some interpreters have tried to claim that Christ had to have been born a creature in order to be the firstborn of all creation, and therefore He is merely a creature, not divine — a line of logic used by Arian heretics such as modern-day Jehovah's Witnesses. However, this interpretation misunderstands that "firstborn" in the Scriptures does not necessarily refer to birth order, but indicates a legal status regarding the one who would inherit the major share of a father's property.

Certain Old Testament passages can help explain the meaning of Christ as firstborn:

- ✠ In Exodus 4:22, Moses says to Pharaoh, "Thus says the Lord, Israel is my firstborn son." What makes this text intriguing is that Israel (earlier known as Jacob) was actually born second, after his older twin brother Esau (Genesis 25:25–26). He came to be considered the firstborn because Esau sold him his birthright for a bowl of lentil soup (Genesis 25:29–34). That meant that Jacob, rather than his biologically older brother, Esau, would have the right to inherit two-thirds of his father's property as the presently putative "firstborn." God recognized this change of status in this passage from Exodus.
- ✠ In another reference recognized as prophetic of the Messiah, God says, "And I will make him the first-born, the highest of the kings of the earth" (Psalm 89:27). This shows that "firstborn" is a messianic title bestowed by God rather than an indication of birth order.

After establishing Christ's credentials as firstborn, Paul goes on to say that all things are created through Him, including the material universe and the immaterial, invisible angelic choirs, four of which are named here. Incidentally, John's prologue teaches the same thing when it says, "All things were made through him, and without him was not anything made that was made" (John 1:3). Further evidence of Christ's credentials are His existence before all things (see also John 1:1–3 regarding the Word's existence in the beginning) and His ability to hold all the things of creation together.

Having established Christ's authority over creation, Paul then turns to Christ's role in redemption: He is head of the Church and the first-born from the dead (Colossians 1:18).

The last sentence brings together two crucial elements underlying Paul's theology of Christ's redemptive death on the Cross: first, that the fullness of God dwells in Christ. While Philippians 2:6–11 says that Christ did not cling to being equal to God but was exalted as Lord after the Resurrection, Colossians explicitly proclaims that the fullness of God dwells in Him. Acknowledging the fullness of God in Christ then moves Paul to the theology of the Cross: Jesus Christ, God incarnate, Creator of all, reconciles all to Himself and makes peace by shedding His blood on the Cross. Here the fullness of God in Christ, through His dying on the Cross, reconciles the world to God.

B. Colossians 1:19–20

> 19 For in him all the fullness of God was pleased to dwell,
> 20 and through him to reconcile to himself all things,
> whether on earth or in heaven, making peace by the
> blood of his cross.

These verses are essential for understanding the necessity of Christ's death on the Cross for human redemption. We begin with the principle that a sin or offense acquires its seriousness from the importance of the person offended, rather than from the one who commits the offense (e.g., hitting an ordinary citizen is not as serious a crime as striking the President of the United States, which is a federal crime). Therefore, sinning against God acquires an infinite and eternal quality because God is infinite and eternal. We humans are mere creatures incapable of making up for an infinite or eternal crime, so we need an infinite and eternal redeemer. Christ is that infinite redeemer, in that the fullness of God resides in Him as He hung upon the Cross to reconcile us. Therefore, He can make up for offenses we can never undo by ourselves. Additionally, it is possible for Him to reconcile all creatures in all places at all time, since the divine nature of Christ has no limits of any kind.

> "Whoever does not seek the cross of Christ doesn't seek the glory of Christ."
>
> — St. John of the Cross

INVESTIGATE

The choirs of angels are mentioned in a variety of passages in Scripture. Look up the following passages and list which of the choirs of angels are named.

PASSAGE	CHOIR(S) OF ANGELS
Isaiah 62:6	
Genesis 3:24	
2 Samuel 22:11	
Exodus 25:18ff	
Ezekiel 1:5–3:10	

PASSAGE	CHOIR(S) OF ANGELS
Colossians 1:16	
Colossians 2:15	
Ephesians 1:21	
Romans 8:38	
Ephesians 3:10	
Ephesians 6:12	
Colossians 2:10	
1 Peter 3:22	

STUDY

A. Colossians 1:21–23

> [21]And you, who once were estranged and hostile in mind, doing evil deeds, [22]he has now reconciled in his body of flesh by his death, in order to present you holy and blameless and irreproachable before him, [23]provided that you continue in the faith, stable and steadfast, not shifting from the hope of the gospel which you heard, which has been preached to every creature under heaven, and of which I, Paul, became a minister.

Paul now addresses both the community and the individual. Apparently, the community was composed of people who had been at odds with each other prior to their conversion. Christ's death on the Cross has brought about a true reconciliation among them. However, they still needed to become holy and blameless, since holiness and blamelessness are not guaranteed by the reconciliation. Rather, each Christian must continue in the faith and hope presented in the gospel. These virtues are the same ones that Paul had previously taught in letters to the Galatians and Romans as necessary for salvation.

B. Colossians 1:24–26

> [24]Now I rejoice in my sufferings for your sake, and in my flesh I complete what is lacking in Christ's afflictions for the sake of his body, that is, the church, [25]of which I became a minister according to the divine office which was given to me for you, to make the word of God fully known, [26]the mystery hidden for ages and generations but now made manifest to his saints.

Next, Paul turns to his own personal experience to reveal another level of meaning in the Cross. As in 2 Corinthians, he refers to his own sufferings but also offers a deeper reflection on them. He can rejoice in suffering because it fills up something still missing in the sufferings of Christ. This does not imply that Christ's death was unable to reconcile the whole world. Rather, this text must be understood in light of Paul's teaching that Christ is the head of His body, the Church.

> *i* In light of Paul's teaching on the power of suffering, we can better understand the role of voluntary suffering—such as in fasting and abstaining—as well as involuntary suffering, as in the case of diseases and accidents. Neither type of suffering is meaningless. We can unite our pain to the Cross of Jesus Christ, particularly by freely making an offering of our suffering (see Romans 12:1). This is particularly effective during Mass, when a spiritual offering at the Offertory allows Christ to unite our suffering with His on the Cross during the Consecration.

The Church is that Body of Christ in which Paul suffers in union with Jesus. As a member of the Church, he makes up for what is lacking in the sufferings of the Body of Christ. Yet, he does so for the sake of Christ's Body, the Church. He clearly understands that his suffering has a greater purpose, and even an effectiveness, for other persons. In some way known only to God, Paul's suffering helps the rest of the Church. Furthermore, it helps in the proclamation of the gospel. This means that his suffering (and ours) either helps open up opportunities to preach the gospel or softens the hearts of those people who might hear the proclamation and become converted — or, most likely, both.

C. Colossians 2:9–15

> [9]For in him the whole fullness of deity dwells bodily,
> [10]and you have come to fullness of life in him, who is
> the head of all rule and authority. [11]In him also you were
> circumcised with a circumcision made without hands,
> by putting off the body of flesh in the circumcision of
> Christ; [12]and you were buried with him in baptism, in
> which you were also raised with him through faith in
> the working of God, who raised him from the dead.
> [13]And you, who were dead in trespasses and the un-
> circumcision of your flesh, God made alive together
> with him, having forgiven us all our trespasses, [14]having
> canceled the bond which stood against us with its legal
> demands; this he set aside, nailing it to the cross. [15]He
> disarmed the principalities and powers and made a
> public example of them, triumphing over them in him.

This section begins by reasserting the fullness of deity dwelling in Christ, the head of all "rule and authority"—another reference to the angelic powers of 1:16. Here, it is connected to a promise that Christians share in a fullness of life in Christ. The means of receiving this fullness of life is through a "circumcision" in Christ—in other words, Baptism. Baptism is more powerful than circumcision, which simply removed flesh, because Baptism is union in faith with Christ's death, burial, and Resurrection.

As Paul discussed in Romans, Baptism can be understood only in light of Christ's death on the Cross and His Resurrection. Just as God's power was made manifest by raising the crucified Jesus back to life, so also does God make us sinners alive again after our having been dead in our trespasses. Further connection yet is made with Christ's Cross through the image of a written document, or "bond," which lists our sins. Paul uses the symbol of such a bond being nailed to the Cross to show that the lawful demand for punishment of sinners was abolished when Christ died on the Cross.

Furthermore, the Cross is the source of power by which Christ disarmed and overcame the angelic "powers" and "principalities" that were apparently part of the angelic host belonging to Satan's rebellion against God. Though Christ's Cross appeared to be a defeat in human viewpoints, it was in fact the great triumph over sin and the evil powers of the angelic realm.

Therefore, the attitude of the believer must be to place even greater trust in the Cross of Christ in order to have any and all sins forgiven, receive the new fullness of life that God desires to bestow on us, and be safe from the spiritual powers that oppose God and seek the destruction of souls.

> Stop here and read
> Colossians 3:1–4:6.

These chapters help us better understand the fullness of life that flows from the power of Christ's death on the Cross and His Resurrection. Christ, who is raised above all, is the one who directs our attention above all. However, also note that it is necessary to die with Christ through Baptism in order to live out this new fullness of life.

D. Colossians 3:1–15

> [1]If then you have been raised with Christ, seek the
> things that are above, where Christ is, seated at the
> right hand of God. [2]Set your minds on things that are
> above, not on things that are on earth. [3]For you have
> died, and your life is hid with Christ in God. [4]When

> Christ who is our life appears, then you also will appear with him in glory.
>
> 5Put to death therefore what is earthly in you: immorality, impurity, passion, evil desire, and covetousness, which is idolatry. 6On account of these the wrath of God is coming. 7In these you once walked, when you lived in them. 8But now put them all away: anger, wrath, malice, slander, and foul talk from your mouth. 9Do not lie to one another, seeing that you have put off the old nature with its practices 10and have put on the new nature, which is being renewed in knowledge after the image of its creator. 11Here there cannot be Greek and Jew, circumcised and uncircumcised, barbarian, Scyth'ian, slave, free man, but Christ is all, and in all.
>
> 12Put on then, as God's chosen ones, holy and beloved, compassion, kindness, lowliness, meekness, and patience, 13forbearing one another and, if one has a complaint against another, forgiving each other; as the Lord has forgiven you, so you also must forgive.
>
> 14And above all these put on love, which binds everything together in perfect harmony. 15 And let the peace of Christ rule in your hearts, to which indeed you were called in the one body. And be thankful.

This section begins with the victory of those who have been raised in Christ. If the baptized are raised with Him, then the goal of life needs to be set on heavenly things, since Christ is in Heaven, seated at the right hand of God the Father. However, if one is to turn one's attention to heavenly things, then it is necessary to live out that aspect of Baptism by which the believer dies to earthly realities. Covetous desire, anger and its manifestations in human speech, and sexual desire that is outside the realm of God's grace, must all be removed like pieces of clothing. This process of spiritual transformation is like the crucifixion, including the removal of clothes and death. However, this spiritual union with Christ's Crucifixion is oriented to a positive transformation in virtue.

INVESTIGATE

Colossians 3:12–15 describes the various virtues that the fullness of life in Christ will bring about. Read these verses and write out the listed virtues.

PASSAGE	VIRTUE
Colossians 3:12	
Colossians 3:13	
Colossians 3:14	
Colossians 3:15	

Paul intended Colossians 3:1–15 to be used as an examination of conscience. Which vices do you still need put to death and which virtues do you need to bring to life? Ask God for the grace to make this transformation, since the point of this passage is to place ourselves under the power of God's grace, available through the death and Resurrection of Jesus Christ. We humans are powerless to make ourselves virtuous, but if we desire the grace of God to transform us, He will give that grace through its one and only source — the death of Jesus on the Cross and His glorious Resurrection from the dead.

DISCUSS

1. How do you think Paul's imprisonment influenced his message to the Philippians?
2. Read Philippians 2:1–11. What implications does this passage have for your life?
3. What does it mean to you that Jesus has the power to redeem all of the cosmos? Do you think that any part of the universe besides our Earth needs to be redeemed?
4. What new things did you learn about angels from this study? What misconceptions about angels are common in modern culture?
5. How can we offer God a sacrifice of love? Why does God want such a sacrifice?
6. Paul says, "Set your minds on things that are above, not on things that are on earth." How, in a practical way, can you do this in your everyday life?

PRACTICE

Using Colossians 3:1–15 as a starting point, make an examination of conscience and then go to Confession.

Session Six

YOU AND THE CROSS

How Paul's Teachings Can Change Your Life

CONSIDER

Paul's letter to the Ephesians is his great letter to the Church, and hence to all of us. It does not appear to be a response to problems that Paul felt a need to correct. Some scholars consider it to be a theological treatise covering certain themes of theology that Paul felt were important. Some hold that this may have been a text for the newly baptized members of the community. Whatever his purpose may have been, Paul gives a wonderful view of the Christian mystery and its impact on the believers' lives. Its vision is essential in allowing Paul's teaching to change our lives.

STUDY

A. Ephesians 1:3–14

> 3Blessed be the God and Father of our Lord Jesus Christ,
> who has blessed us in Christ with every spiritual bless-
> ing in the heavenly places, 4even as he chose us in him
> before the foundation of the world, that we should be
> holy and blameless before him. 5He destined us in love
> to be his sons through Jesus Christ, according to the
> purpose of his will, 6to the praise of his glorious grace

> which he freely bestowed on us in the Beloved. [7]In him we have redemption through his blood, the forgiveness of our trespasses, according to the riches of his grace [8]which he lavished upon us. [9]For he has made known to us in all wisdom and insight the mystery of his will, according to his purpose which he set forth in Christ [10]as a plan for the fullness of time, to unite all things in him, things in heaven and things on earth.
>
> [11]In him, according to the purpose of him who accomplishes all things according to the counsel of his will, [12]we who first hoped in Christ have been destined and appointed to live for the praise of his glory. [13]In him you also, who have heard the word of truth, the gospel of your salvation, and have believed in him, were sealed with the promised Holy Spirit, [14]who is the guarantee of our inheritance until we acquire possession of it, to the praise of his glory.

Ephesians starts off with a hymn about the preeminence of Jesus Christ. As do many of the Psalms and the *Benedictus* of St. Zechariah (Luke 1:68), it begins by proclaiming God as blessed. The reason God is so obviously blessed is that He has blessed us in Christ with every spiritual blessing — which is the preeminence of Christ.

> Being "sealed with the Holy Spirit" refers to the effect of the Holy Spirit on the soul when it is received in Baptism and Confirmation.

Among these blessings is our transformation into God's children. Another is our redemption, which is the forgiveness of sins. However, as is always true of Paul, this redemption comes through the shedding of Christ's blood, a free gift bestowed only at the high cost of Jesus' death on the Cross.

While this mystery of God's will was made known in wisdom and insight, it is received by those who hear the word of truth — which is this gospel of salvation in Jesus Christ — and believe in it, and are sealed with the Holy Spirit.

B. Ephesians 2:13–22

> 13 But now in Christ Jesus you who once were far off have
> been brought near in the blood of Christ. 14 For he is
> our peace, who has made us both one, and has broken
> down the dividing wall of hostility, 15 by abolishing in
> his flesh the law of commandments and ordinances, that
> he might create in himself one new man in place of the
> two, so making peace, 16 and might reconcile us both to
> God in one body through the cross, thereby bringing
> the hostility to an end. 17 And he came and preached
> peace to you who were far off and peace to those who
> were near; 18 for through him we both have access in
> one Spirit to the Father. 19 So then you are no longer
> strangers and sojourners, but you are fellow citizens
> with the saints and members of the household of God,
> 20 built upon the foundation of the apostles and prophets,
> Christ Jesus himself being the cornerstone, 21 in whom
> the whole structure is joined together and grows into
> a holy temple in the Lord; 22 in whom you also are built
> into it for a dwelling place of God in the Spirit.

This section of Ephesians addresses the hostility that existed between Jews and Gentiles. The Gentiles are those who were far off, divided from Jews by a "dividing wall of hostility." Mere human efforts could not overcome the differences that separated Jews and Gentiles on strong, irreconcilable religious principles. However, Jesus' death on the Cross, when He shed His blood and died in the flesh, was able to abolish the "law of commandments and ordinances." This law kept Jews from certain forms of association with Gentiles and led them to consider Gentiles as morally and spiritually inferior. On the other hand, Gentiles could easily consider Jews to be disloyal to the government, because they would not take part in the local military (the soldiers had to pay homage to pagan deities) or government (Jews were exempt from taxes that supported not only the government but the local temples).

Paul's point is that Jesus Christ is the one capable of breaking down these barriers by shedding His blood and dying on the Cross. His death on the Cross put salvation on a completely different basis than either Judaism or paganism. The law was abolished by His death; faith in Him, not the law, unites sinners to Him. Diverse peoples with irreconcilable religions could be reconciled with God, and thereby end their hostility. In fact, through the Cross they are brought into one body, the Church. In the context of that reconciliation, Christ could evangelize (the Greek word translated as "preach" is the verb "evangelize") both to the Gentiles, who were far away, and to the Jews, who were closer (2:17).

> *i* Another aspect of 2:16–17 connects Christ's death on the cross with Jewish ideas of sacrifice. The word *Korban,* a common Jewish term for a sacrifice that Jesus mentions in Mark 7:11, comes from the root meaning "bring near." A sacrifice is something that the human brings near to the altar, and it is something by which a human is drawn nearer to God. The claim that Christ's Cross and preaching brings the Gentiles "near" may well be an underlying idea in Paul's mind.

This was even possible because the reconciliation He effected between God and sinful humanity gave the converted believers access to God the Father in the power of the Holy Spirit. In other words, Christ's death effected an interpersonal communion with God, who, as the Trinity revealed by Jesus Christ, is also interpersonal at the same time He is one God.

This reconciliation makes Christians into members of a single household of God. This house has the prophets and apostles as its foundation, and Jesus Christ as its cornerstone (2:20). This household is a temple in which God, the only true God, dwells and is adored. This image of the temple also brings out the importance of communion with God, since the temple was the place to meet God.

> *i* The image of this spiritual temple is connected with the Temple in Jerusalem. The temple itself was built on top of a hill, the "Temple Mount." When Herod the Great began rebuilding the temple around 19 B.C., he first constructed an outer retaining wall around the hill, thereby squaring it off. This is the modern "Wailing Wall," or "Western Wall," as Jews prefer to call it. The foundations of this wall are precisely cut ashlar-style blocks, weighing 20 to 60 tons each. These would be a symbol of the prophets and the apostles. In the center of the wall are two enormous blocks, weighing about 450 tons. Herod had them placed there to absorb the shock of the periodic earthquakes in the region. They saved the wall from collapse many times—the way Jesus Christ, the "keystone," keeps the Church from collapsing.

INVESTIGATE

Ephesians 2:14–16 contains a number of features that seem based on the hymn found in Colossians 1:15–20, which also praises Christ who brings peace and reconciliation to the world. Look back on the Colossians text and find key elements that appear in Ephesians 2:14–16. This connection, among many others, shows that these two epistles may well have been written at the same time and perhaps were even sent in the same mail packet to the different communities of Asia Minor (modern Turkey).

STUDY

A. Ephesians 5:1–5

> 1Therefore be imitators of God, as beloved children.
> 2And walk in love, as Christ loved us and gave himself up
> for us, a fragrant offering and sacrifice to God. 3But im-
> morality and all impurity or covetousness must not even
> be named among you, as is fitting among saints. 4Let
> there be no filthiness, nor silly talk, nor levity, which
> are not fitting; but instead let there be thanksgiving. 5Be
> sure of this, that no immoral or impure man, or one who
> is covetous (that is, an idolater), has any inheritance in
> the kingdom of Christ and of God.

This section is part of the moral exhortation in Ephesians that connects the life of virtue with Christ's death on the Cross. As is typical of Paul's teaching, Christ's death on the Cross is seen as a sacrifice to God. However, instead of his usual point — that this sacrifice frees sinners, as the only acceptable offering to God — here, Paul urges Christians to love in a sacrificial way. He stresses that just as Jesus gave Himself up for us, so must we give ourselves up for one another.

> The word "Eucharist" means "thanksgiving."

The concrete meaning of this sacrifice is spelled out when Paul calls us away from sexual immorality and covetousness. Giving up these desires is one aspect of the sacrifice. Also, as was typical of many Israelite sacrifices, the offering of thanksgiving was included. In fact, thanksgiving sacrifices were one category of Israelite sacrifices.

B. Ephesians 5:25–27

> 25Husbands, love your wives, as Christ loved the church
> and gave himself up for her, 26that he might sanctify her,
> having cleansed her by the washing of water with the
> word, 27that he might present the church to himself in
> splendor, without spot or wrinkle or any such thing,
> that she might be holy and without blemish.

The command Paul gives to husbands to love their wives is connected with Christ's sacrifice on the Cross, where He gave Himself up for His bride, the Church. In this passage, Paul encourages one particular group to live out a sacrificial love modeled on Christ's sacrifice of Himself on the Cross.

CONSIDER

I began this study of Paul's teaching on Jesus' death on the Cross with a desire to simply let the texts speak. I did not have an overarching theory before I began the study, though I did assume the Catholic Faith as the basis for my desire to read these texts and believe them. Because I am a Catholic, I trust the long history of the Church's interpretation of these epistles as a source for the meaning of life. I believe the Church's claim that the Holy Spirit inspired Paul to write his letters, and therefore I read them as authoritative for my faith and the very meaning of my life.

Another aspect of my approach comes from my training in biblical exegesis. I wanted the texts to speak for themselves, and I wanted their cumulative effect to come from within the structures, forms of speech, vocabulary, and historical background of the texts. The texts address themselves to the reader and evoke a response and a meaning. However, both because these texts are very rich on the human level, and, I believe, are inspired at a divine level, they present great depth of meaning and a variety of interpretations.

This study focused on the power of the Cross as Paul understood it. Looking at his writings as a whole, I saw several important points emerge.

- Paul teaches often about the death of Jesus on the Cross. His letters contain a wide number of passages, usually multiple texts in any one letter, that treat some aspect of his theology of the Cross.
- The majority of Paul's autobiographical texts are linked to his teaching of the Cross. Whether in 2 Corinthians, Galatians, or Philippians, Paul tells the reader about his personal and ethnic background, his life as a Christian, and his misadventures and suffering in connection with his theology of the Crucifixion of Jesus Christ. It seems easy to conclude that Paul understood his life in terms of Jesus Christ crucified. That is why he can proclaim so readily, "It is no longer I who live, but Christ who lives in me" (Galatians 2:20). At the same time, he relates these episodes not to satisfy the reader's curiosity about his life — in fact, scholars' curiosity about his biography is piqued by these snippets — but, rather, to illustrate a particular aspect of his theology of the Cross.

- ✠ Paul repeatedly teaches that Christ's death on the Cross is to be interpreted in the light of Israelite sacrifices: Passover (1 Corinthians 5:7), the Day of Atonement (Romans 3:25), and sin offerings in general (2 Corinthians 2:21). Naturally, he views Christ through the lenses of the Judaism in which he was raised, but then he goes beyond any standard Jewish expectations by interpreting Christ's death as a sacrifice for sin. Human sacrifice was forbidden in Judaism, yet Paul proclaims that Jesus' death on the Cross is the only sacrifice that can bring true reconciliation with God. This is shocking to Jewish sensitivities, the same sensitivities that Paul himself once held so powerfully.

- ✠ Paul is emphatic that Christ's death saves sinners from sin. It is a powerful reality that can transform lives.

- ✠ The death of Christ is the essential fact of a new covenant. The old covenant had been abrogated, as Jeremiah and Ezekiel had proclaimed at the time of the sixth century B.C. Exile into Babylon. Yet both prophets foretold a new covenant. It was Christ Himself who announced that He fulfilled it. For that reason Paul argued in Galatians, Romans, and Philippians that the righteousness that came from observing the Law was replaced by the righteousness that Christ won by His death on the Cross. The whole argument about circumcision hinges on Paul's understanding of the new covenant effected on the Cross, rather than the old covenant created at Sinai.

- ✠ A number of times Paul states that Jesus Christ who died on the Cross is also God. In the earlier letters, the references to Christ's divinity are more oblique, since all Jews were trained in a radically strict monotheism. Speaking of God's Son was very difficult, therefore, since it might seem to contradict faith in God's oneness. Yet by the time Paul includes hymns in his letters (Philippians, Colossians, and Ephesians), the profession of Christ's Divinity is more explicit and forthright. The significance of teaching that God's Son died on the Cross is to make the results of the Cross available to people of all places and all eras of history. Jesus, the Son of God, died to save all humanity throughout all time. This is possible precisely because Jesus is the infinite and eternal God who died within time to redeem humanity from eternal death.

✠ Since Jesus is God and possesses true eternity in His divine nature, the Cross and its power are perpetually available throughout all time. Paul understands that the Cross is the center of the sacraments. Both he and our Lord teach that all the sacraments are rooted in the Cross. For instance, when you are baptized, you are baptized into the death of Jesus so you can rise with Him. It is only through conformity to Christ's death and Resurrection that we obtain their power and grace. Therefore, Christ's Divinity must also be kept in mind as Paul teaches about the sacraments and their connection to the Cross and Resurrection.

INVESTIGATE

Read the following passages from Paul's letters and note some of the key concepts about the sacraments.

PASSAGE	KEY CONCEPT/SACRAMENT
Ephesians 4:1–13	

PASSAGE	KEY CONCEPT/SACRAMENT
Colossians 2:8–15	
Titus 3:4–7	
2 Corinthians 2:5–11	
2 Corinthians 5:18–21	
Ephesians 1:13–14	
Ephesians 4:30	
Acts 2:41–47	
Acts 20:7–11	

PASSAGE	KEY CONCEPT/SACRAMENT
I Timothy 3:1–7	
I Corinthians 7:1–6	

> Faith is to believe what you do not see; the reward of this faith is to see what you believe.
>
> —St. Augustine

CONSIDER

Paul explains that because we are crucified with Christ, we no longer live, but Christ lives through us. The very meaning of our lives comes now from the Cross. We have been crucified with Christ in order that we might live with Him. It is no longer I who live, but Christ who lives in me. My flesh is what needs to die — my ego trip, my egomania — so that Christ can live in me.

It's a process. But if we don't focus on the Cross and what it means to die to ourselves, then we will never live with Christ.

Paul's examination of the death of Christ on the Cross provides us with several important lessons that are essential to our life as Christians.

The death of Christ on the Cross is a model for human behavior, since Christ died because He loved sinners while they were still sinners (Romans 5:8). He loved the unlovely and even the unlovable, loving sinners infinitely. He truly loves humanity to death. This complete outpouring of love is the model for all human love, whether in marriage or in the Church.

Christ's death is both a source of grace by which sinners overcome the tendency to sin in life and the model for overcoming actual sin. Sinners must die to sin in order to cease doing what is wrong. By dying to sin, they can put on virtue, much as Christ put on a glorified body in His Resurrection.

Christ's death offers the only hope that can save human beings. It gives meaning to suffering in this life, because humans can unite their own suffering with that of Christ's pain and suffering on the Cross. Therefore, suffering and even apparent failure, such as Paul in his own life and mission, do not lead to despair. Instead, by uniting this suffering to Christ's Cross, our suffering will lead to a glory like Christ's in the Resurrection.

Finally, by His death Christ conquered death itself. This gives us hope that death will not be our final end. We will not be annihilated into some meaningless nothingness. Rather, Christ defeated His enemy, death (1 Corinthians 15:26), and rose triumphant over it. In turn, He will raise up to eternal life those who believe in the power of His Cross to forgive sin, who allow it to transform them into loving, hoping, redeemed believers. Beyond the Cross is the hope of resurrection.

DISCUSS

1. Jesus said to take up our cross and follow Him. What is your cross? Are you resisting it or accepting it? How can you accept it more graciously?

2. How can you help others accept their crosses?

3. How do you relate the Mass to the Cross?

4. In what ways are the other sacraments intrinsically linked to the Cross as well?

5. What part of Paul's teachings about the power of the Cross has had the most meaning and impact for your life? How will you live differently from now on?

PRACTICE

This week, as you attend Mass, enter fully into the representation of Calvary, accepting Jesus' death on behalf of your sins. Spend some time before the Blessed Sacrament, giving thanks for the gift of the Cross and the changes that Christ's sacrifice has created in your life. Renew your commitment to living a life charged and changed by the power of the Cross.

APPENDIX

Reading Checklist for the Apostle Paul

The letters of St. Paul present us with a unique opportunity to focus on the writings and teachings of the Apostle to the Gentiles. The following checklist is a suggested reading plan that you can use to read through all of St. Paul's letters in ninety-eight days and, as a bonus, the passages dealing with his life in the Acts of the Apostles in another thirty-six days.

1. ___ Romans 1
2. ___ Romans 2:1–3:8
3. ___ Romans 3:9–31
4. ___ Romans 4
5. ___ Romans 5
6. ___ Romans 6
7. ___ Romans 7
8. ___ Romans 8:1–17
9. ___ Romans 8:18–39
10. ___ Romans 9:1–29
11. ___ Romans 9:30–10:13
12. ___ Romans 10:14–21
13. ___ Romans 11:1–16
14. ___ Romans 11:17–36
15. ___ Romans 12
16. ___ Romans 13
17. ___ Romans 14
18. ___ Romans 15:1–13
19. ___ Romans 15:14–33
20. ___ Romans 16
21. ___ I Corinthians 1
22. ___ I Corinthians 2
23. ___ I Corinthians 3
24. ___ I Corinthians 4

25. ___ 1 Corinthians 5
26. ___ 1 Corinthians 6
27. ___ 1 Corinthians 7:1–24
28. ___ 1 Corinthians 7:25–40
29. ___ 1 Corinthians 8
30. ___ 1 Corinthians 9
31. ___ 1 Corinthians 10:1–13
32. ___ 1 Corinthians 10:14–11:1
33. ___ 1 Corinthians 11:2–16
34. ___ 1 Corinthians 11:17–34
35. ___ 1 Corinthians 12
36. ___ 1 Corinthians 13
37. ___ 1 Corinthians 14:1–25
38. ___ 1 Corinthians 14:26–40
39. ___ 1 Corinthians 15:1–34
40. ___ 1 Corinthians 15:35–58
41. ___ 1 Corinthians 16
42. ___ 2 Corinthians 1:1–22
43. ___ 2 Corinthians 1:23–2:17
44. ___ 2 Corinthians 3
45. ___ 2 Corinthians 4:1–15
46. ___ 2 Corinthians 4:16–5:17
47. ___ 2 Corinthians 5:18–7:1
48. ___ 2 Corinthians 7:2–16
49. ___ 2 Corinthians 8
50. ___ 2 Corinthians 9
51. ___ 2 Corinthians 10
52. ___ 2 Corinthians 11:1–21
53. ___ 2 Corinthians 11:22–33
54. ___ 2 Corinthians 12
55. ___ 2 Corinthians 13
56. ___ Galatians 1
57. ___ Galatians 2
58. ___ Galatians 3:1–4:7
59. ___ Galatians 4:8–31
60. ___ Galatians 5
61. ___ Galatians 6
62. ___ Ephesians 1
63. ___ Ephesians 2
64. ___ Ephesians 3
65. ___ Ephesians 4:1–16
66. ___ Ephesians 4:17–5:21
67. ___ Ephesians 5:22–6:9
68. ___ Ephesians 6:10–24
69. ___ Philippians 1
70. ___ Philippians 2
71. ___ Philippians 3:1–4:1
72. ___ Philippians 4:2–23

73. ____ Colossians 1
74. ____ Colossians 2
75. ____ Colossians 3
76. ____ Colossians 4
77. ____ 1 Thessalonians 1
78. ____ 1 Thessalonians 2
79. ____ 1 Thessalonians 3
80. ____ 1 Thessalonians 4
81. ____ 1 Thessalonians 5
82. ____ 2 Thessalonians 1
83. ____ 2 Thessalonians 2
84. ____ 2 Thessalonians 3
85. ____ 1 Timothy 1
86. ____ 1 Timothy 2
87. ____ 1 Timothy 3
88. ____ 1 Timothy 4
89. ____ 1 Timothy 5
90. ____ 1 Timothy 6
91. ____ 2 Timothy 1
92. ____ 2 Timothy 2
93. ____ 2 Timothy 3
94. ____ 2 Timothy 4
95. ____ Titus 1
96. ____ Titus 2
97. ____ Titus 3
98. ____ Philemon

BONUS

St. Paul in Acts of the Apostles

99. ___ Acts 6
100. ___ Acts 7:1–22
101. ___ Acts 7:23–43
102. ___ Acts 7:44–8:2
103. ___ Acts 8:3–25
104. ___ Acts 8:26–40
105. ___ Acts 9:1–20
106. ___ Acts 9:21–43
107. ___ Acts 10:1–24
108. ___ Acts 11
109. ___ Acts 12
110. ___ Acts 13:1–25
111. ___ Acts 13:26–52
112. ___ Acts 14:1–15:5
113. ___ Acts 15:6–21
114. ___ Acts 15:22–41
115. ___ Acts 16:1–21
116. ___ Acts 16:22–40
117. ___ Acts 17:1–15
118. ___ Acts 17:16–34
119. ___ Acts 18
120. ___ Acts 19:1–20
121. ___ Acts 19:21–40
122. ___ Acts 20:1–16
123. ___ Acts 20:17–38
124. ___ Acts 21:1–14
125. ___ Acts 21:15–36
126. ___ Acts 21:37–22:29
127. ___ Acts 22:30–23:10
128. ___ Acts 23:11–35
129. ___ Acts 24
130. ___ Acts 25
131. ___ Acts 26
132. ___ Acts 27:1–26
133. ___ Acts 27:27–44
134. ___ Acts 28

A PRAYER TO THE APOSTLE PAUL

Glorious St. Paul,
most zealous apostle,
martyr for the love of Christ,
give us a deep faith,
a steadfast hope,
a burning love for our Lord,
so that we can proclaim with you,
"It is no longer I who live, but Christ who lives in me."

Help us to become apostles,
serving the Church with a pure heart,
witnesses to her truth and beauty
amidst the darkness of our days.
With you we praise God, our Father:
"To him be the glory, in the Church and in Christ,
now and for ever."
Amen.

Notes

Notes

Notes

Notes

Notes

Notes

Notes